Penguin Books
The F-Plan Calorie and Fibre Chart

Audrey Eyton is the author of the sensational bestseller *The F-Plan* which has inspired millions of slimmers. She can justly claim to have invented that now popular feature of every magazine stall – the slimming magazine. When she and her partner founded *Slimming Magazine* twelve years ago it was the first publication in the world to specialize in the subject. The magazine was started as a 'cottage industry', on practically no capital, because no one else believed there was enough to write on the subject, regularly. How wrong they were! The magazine was an instant success and has continued to be the dominating bestseller despite the many rival publications which have followed.

For many years Audrey Eyton edited the magazine herself, and later became Editorial Director. During their years of ownership (the company was sold in 1980) she and her partner also started Ragdale Hall Health Farm and founded and developed one of Britain's largest chains of slimming clubs. Mrs Eyton continues to work as a consultant to the company.

During her many years of specialization in this subject, Mrs Eyton has worked with most of the world's leading nutritional, medical and psychological experts. No writer has a greater knowledge and understanding of the subject. She has become an expert in her own right.

She has a fifteen-year-old son, and lives in Kensington and Kent.

Audrey Eyton

The F-Plan Calorie and Fibre Chart

Charts compiled and recipes devised by
Joyce Hughes, B.Sc.

Research directed by Dr Elizabeth Evans

Penguin Books

f-plan calorie counter disk N5 file 02 sw

Penguin Books Ltd, Harmondsworth, Middlesex, England
Penguin Books, 625 Madison Avenue, New York, New York 10022, U.S.A.
Penguin Books Australia Ltd, Ringwood, Victoria, Australia
Penguin Books Canada Ltd, 2801 John Street, Markham, Ontario, Canada L3R 1B4
Penguin Books (N Z.) Ltd, 182 190 Wairau Road, Auckland 10, New Zealand

First published 1982
Reprinted 1982 (five times), 1983 (eight times)

Copyright © Audrey Eyton, 1982
All rights reserved

Made and printed in Great Britain by
Richard Clay (The Chaucer Press) Ltd,
Bungay, Suffolk
Filmset in Monophoto Times by
Northumberland Press Ltd, Gateshead

One of the wonderful things about being in the publishing world is the pleasure of working with so many exceptionally nice and highly competent women. I would like to dedicate this book to four of them – Sally Gaminara, Jenny Wilford, Patience Bulkeley and Felicity Green, with thanks to so many more who have helped me over the years.

Contents

As with all slimming diets, if you suffer from any health problems at all, check with your doctor before embarking on a dieting programme.

Acknowledgements

In addition to my excellent collaborators, Joyce Hughes and Elizabeth Evans, I would like to express my warmest gratitude to Dr David Southgate of the Food Research Institute, to Derek Miller of London University's Department of Nutrition and to Dr Martin Eastwood of the Western General Hospital, Edinburgh, all of whom have been most generous with their help and encouragement. My thanks, too, to Sue Horsman, without whose supersonic typing I would never reach a deadline, and to my son Matthew who, even when I delve into the sombre depths of the lower intestine, can always be relied on to come up with the jokes.

Preface

In the early spring of 1982, Linda Cook, one of the volunteers who had agreed to test a highly unusual new slimming diet, revisited London University's Department of Nutrition for her first week's weight check. Linda, who is Matron of the Royal Leamington Spa Nursing Home, hadn't told her own staff that she was on a diet because . . . well, frankly, she had great doubts about whether she was losing any weight on it.

She had been eating meals like baked beans on toast and foods like baked potatoes. That was what – to her great surprise – she had been told to eat and she had followed instructions precisely. But after years of being indoctrinated, along with the rest of the British public, with the idea that such foods were 'fattening' she retained some of her doubts.

An even greater cause of doubt about her weight loss was the fact that she didn't feel at all hungry. Previous dieting regimes had always been accompanied by that 'half empty' feeling which this time was strangely lacking. She found it hard to imagine that she could be shedding weight without it. So it was with little optimism that she stepped on the scales to be weighed by Dr Elizabeth Evans, who was supervising the diet trials at the University.

Linda had lost 8lb in her first week on the F-Plan.

The following week she shed a further 5lb.

By the end of the third week she was as lean as a greyhound, having shed every one of her 17 surplus pounds of weight.

Linda, along with many other F-Plan dieters on the University's test panel, had shed surplus weight considerably more quickly than ever before, and with an ease which she declared to be 'absolutely staggering'. Her experience, later to be shared by hundreds of thousands of other Britons, demonstrates the F-Plan phenomenon.

The F-Plan diet has literally swept the country. At no time in history have so many Britons been shedding weight on the same diet. During the early weeks, despite herculean efforts by printer and publisher, it was nearly impossible to get *The F-Plan* into the bookshops as speedily as it was being snapped up and borne off by an eager public. The book rapidly became the fastest-selling book in the almost fifty years' history of Penguin Books, selling twice as quickly as the previous record-holder, *Lady Chatterley's Lover*, when her ladyship came off the banned list in the 1960s amid an unprecedented tumult of publicity.

The F-Plan has consistently headed Britain's bestseller lists since it was first published in May. The sensation it has created made front-page news in the *Sunday Times*. It has already sold, in a matter of months, hundreds of thousands more copies than all the American bestsellers put together – Atkins, Scarsdale, Pritikin, Mazel – have sold collectively in Britain over a period of many years. Sales are now approaching the million mark.

Along with the Falklands crisis and the royal baby, *The F-Plan* has been Britain's major talking topic of 1982. It became the subject of a Giles cartoon in the *Daily Express* and of Miles Kington's popular column in *The Times*; it featured in dozens of radio and television programmes and even in the mid-morning banter of Wogan and Young on Radio 2.

The F-Plan has caused 'happenings' that have never been known before in Britain. A near-famine of bran hit the country. Baked beans bounced off the supermarket shelves at such a rate that a puzzled supermarket manager in Bristol phoned the manufacturers to discover 'what on earth was happening'. Shops all over the country painted their windows with the slogan, 'F-Plan ingredients sold here'. A restaurant in Newcastle added F-Plan sandwiches for dieters to its lunchtime menu. So did a works canteen in Middlesex, and found that so many of the staff were following the diet that this became the top-selling lunch. It would be nice to report that even that living personification of slenderness, Twiggy, followed the F-Plan. Not necessary – but we *can* reveal that her husband did!

The F-Plan appeal is universal. TV stations decided to feature it because so many of their own staff were following the diet. Women's page editors of newspapers reported on their own weight loss, and the SDP's Dr David Owen proudly announced his personal F-Plan weight loss of a stone in three weeks.

A duchess was spotted carrying the book and buying in her supplies at the local shop; whole villages and entire offices got together to shed their surplus pounds. A keen-eyed journalist in Scotland sighted a copy on the desk of the portly Lord Provost. And – the author's own favourite story – a company director from Kent phoned to tell her that the vicar, on his regular call, had refused biscuits with his tea because he was on the F-Plan.

Why all the fuss? Why such a sensation? And how was it that a diet-weary public has appreciated, with such perception and alacrity, that the F-Plan is not just another diet, but the start of a complete revolution that has upturned decades of outdated theories on dieting and that will influence slimming methods for decades to come?

The *Daily Express*, swift to spot the significance of the F-Plan, first introduced it to their readers and thus tempted many Britons to give this diet a try. But what happened after that – the enormous build-up of enthusiasm and interest – was a simple multiplication of the Linda Cook story, many thousands of times.

People tried the F-Plan, found they could keep to it, discovered they were losing weight more easily and speedily than ever before, and triumphantly told their friends: 'It works!' And thus the news spread.

The real reason for the F-Plan sensation is summed up in those two words. It works.

In this book you will find a new, even more flexible way of making the F-Plan work to solve your weight problem.

Introduction

Reduce your intake of calories – increase your intake of dietary fibre. That is the basis of the outstanding success of the F-Plan method of dieting.

The F-Plan diet provides slimmers with a wide selection of low-calorie fibre-rich meals from which they can swiftly put together their own daily menus. Now this partner publication, *The F-Plan Calorie and Fibre Chart*, makes it easy for every dieter to devise his or her own meals on the same slimming principles. It adds an extra dimension of eat-your-own-thing freedom to F-Plan dieting.

During the past ten years there has been a complete revolution in medical and nutritional attitudes to the question of which foods are most beneficial in relation to health and weight control. From the results of scientific surveys and experiments in recent years, culminating in the F-Plan dieting method, many of the foods which were previously much underrated on health grounds, and often banned almost completely for slimmers, have been revealed as being of exceptional value on both counts. These foods are the fibre-rich cereal foods, fruit and vegetables – foods like wholemeal bread, bran cereals, potatoes, beans, peas, sweetcorn, even wholemeal pasta.

The F-Plan Calorie and Fibre Chart is the first chart to make it possible to keep to the correct number of calories and, at the same time, to choose the foods which will be of most help in making slimming both easier and speedier. For the health-conscious person, as well as those concerned about weight, it is a unique guide, making it possible to follow that major modern nutritional recommendation made by all leading medical authorities in the Western world: increase your intake of dietary fibre.

The full slimming and health benefits of dietary fibre

cannot be obtained from bran alone, as many health-conscious people used to imagine. Indeed there are some medical experts who advise against an excessive intake of this single fibre-supplying substance. Have a little bran, by all means, but to obtain the full benefit of dietary fibre it is necessary to obtain this valuable substance from a wide range of cereal, fruit and vegetable foods. The exact nature of dietary fibre differs a little from plant to plant. While the major overall benefits of a high-fibre diet are now clearly understood – in making us feel much more full and satisfied on much less food, in aiding our weight loss and speeding waste matter through the bowel to prevent constipation and the major associated bowel diseases – it is thought that different fibre-supplying foods vary in value in their specific helpful functions.

Medical experts suspect, for instance, that the dietary fibre in cereals has a higher overall water-holding capacity than that in an equivalent weight of fruit and vegetables. This means that cereal fibre is particularly effective for the slimmer in filling the stomach, and has a major health function in speeding the passage of waste matter through the bowel.

Fruit and vegetables are thought to be a little less useful in those ways. However, those medical experts who suspect that dietary fibre plays a preventative role in relation to coronary heart disease believe that the fibre in fruit and vegetables may well be of most value in this area.

As many F-Plan dieters have already discovered, high-fibre dieting leads to speedy weight loss. This is partly because fibre-rich foods are less fully digested than other foods. The result is that fewer of the calories consumed are utilized by the body, so that the body has to draw on more of its own surplus fat. However, as dieters indelicate enough to peer down the loo have noted (there are those who complain that the F-Plan has had all Britain looking over its shoulder!), fibre-rich foods are less fully digested than others.

Sweetcorn, for instance, can be detected in near whole and recognizable form in the human faeces. For this reason, nutritionists often use this food to measure transit time – the time it takes for food put in the mouth to pass right through the body.

If a food is passing through the body in such a barely digested form, it is unlikely that the body can be extracting many of those fattening calories from it on the way. So, although calorie charts list cooked sweetcorn kernels at around 35 calories an ounce, it is unlikely that anything approaching that number are really being used by the body.

At some time in the future it will be possible for medical researchers to rate different fibre-rich foods for their varying degrees of digestibility. When this happens, calorie charts as we know them today will almost certainly show many alterations in existing figures. Medical research into dietary fibre, begun only a few years ago, is now thrusting forward as more and more values and virtues of this fascinating material are revealed.

But until more is known, today's message is: Obtain your dietary fibre from as wide a range of unrefined cereals, fruit and vegetable foods as possible in order to ensure the full range of benefits. Yesterday's message of 'bran alone' is now outdated.

The F-Plan Calorie and Fibre Chart provides the information you need to follow this new principle for fitness and weight control.

One of the many factors behind the outstanding success of the F-Plan diet method has been the warmth and enthusiasm with which it has been greeted in the world of science and medicine. After a larger than usual dose of dieting nonsense from overseas during this past year, the F-Plan, a diet based soundly on scientific and medical research, has been welcomed with delight and relief. Professors of nutrition, doctors of medicine and leading researchers in these subjects have endorsed the fact that the F-Plan shows us the way we *should* indeed be eating if we are concerned about health and weight control.

For this reason the most generous expert assistance and co-operation has been given in helping to research and compile this first really comprehensive calorie and fibre guide. Today's enlightened experts realize that there is little point in discovering important diet guidelines unless these can be presented to the public in a form which makes them realistic and easy to incorporate into daily eating.

On this principle, Dr Elizabeth Evans has worked most diligently in supervising research, and Derek Miller, the distinguished nutritional expert, has made research information and facilities available to us at London University. At the Food Research Institute Dr David Southgate, who has made a special study of dietary fibre and whose research is the source of the scientific textbook fibre figures, has provided analytical values for the dietary fibre in a range of usefully fibre-rich canned and packaged foods, so that for the first time these products, which form such a major part of modern eating, can be realistically assessed and used for health value.

Another expert in the work on dietary fibre, Dr Martin Eastwood of Edinburgh's Western General Hospital, has generously given his advice and guidance, and Joyce Hughes, who lectures in nutrition at Croydon College, has undertaken the task of compiling the F-Plan Calorie and Fibre Chart.

We use the word 'chart', but in fact – thanks to all this expert help and co-operation – you will find three food charts in this book (in addition to a calorie chart of drinks) to make it triply easy to follow the new high-fibre low-calorie method of eating for weight reduction and health benefit.

The first makes it easy to see which foods are low in calories and which are high in dietary fibre by listing the calorie and fibre content of average or easily recognizable portions of all the basic foods. You will see at a glance the number of calories and the quantity of dietary fibre (when present) in a whole average-sized eating apple, or a carrot, or a rasher of bacon. We call this chart 'The Instant Calorie and Fibre Guide'.

The Basic Calorie and Fibre Chart, starting on page 127,

reveals the calorie and fibre content (where present) of all those basic everyday foods on a per ounce basis.

Our next chart makes high-fibre low-calorie eating even easier. In this we reveal the number of calories and the quantity of dietary fibre present in useful canned and packaged foods. The use of convenience foods need be no crime in health and weight control if the correct ones are chosen: in fact they can be a great asset. Here is the guide you need.

Switching to this new and better way of eating is much helped by the many ready-planned and calorie- and fibre-counted meals in *The F-Plan* diet book, which can still be obtained from bookshops by the seemingly few Britons who do not own a copy already. In *The F-Plan Calorie and Fibre Chart* we add more meal suggestions to your selection – speedy meals based on manufacturers' packaged high-fibre foods.

Mainly, however, the purpose of this book is to make plan-it-yourself F-Plan meals possible for the first time. On the following pages you will find all the information you need to enjoy the abundant benefits of this new way of eating for slimming and fitness.

1

Boosting fibre intake – how and why

In order to gain the full benefits of the F-Plan method of dieting it is recommended that you consume approximately 35 to 50 grams of dietary fibre daily.

In the calorie charts in this book you will find the fibre content of all the everyday foods, and you will be able to choose your foods to aim at this total. Only cereal food, fruit and vegetables – plant foods as opposed to animal foods – contain dietary fibre, so you will find yourself following a diet containing rather more vegetable foods and a little less of those we think of as protein foods (meat, fish, cheese and eggs) than has probably been your habit in the past.

Is this a bad thing? Most certainly not. The days of the dictum: 'Eat a great big juicy steak for health and fitness' are long past. Modern research has revealed that those once extolled animal foods help to encourage our undoubted over-consumption of fat, with its dire effect on weight and health. Today's nutritional advice does not urge us to become vegetarians, but it takes us to a half-way stage of eating less 'protein food' and more vegetable food.

It even becomes necessary to put in inverted commas that term 'protein food', in its commonly accepted meaning. There is a good deal of protein in many of the fibre-rich vegetable foods like peas, beans, nuts, potatoes and cereals. At one time this protein content was somewhat looked down upon nutritionally and even termed 'second-class protein'. Not so today. Now it is recognized scientifically as being of equal value to the protein obtained from animal sources, provided it is part of a mixed diet.

By increasing fibre intake you automatically cut down

fat intake. Most plant foods have an almost negligible fat content. Thus you find yourself following the two major recommendations for weight control and health: Eat MORE dietary fibre, eat LESS fat.

Notice that the word 'approximately' is used in recommending 35 to 50 grams of dietary fibre daily. When you are following the F-Plan slimming method a high percentage of fibre-rich foods is a valuable factor in the effectiveness of your diet. However, the number of grams of dietary fibre which can be realistically and easily consumed each day will depend to some degree on the number of calories you are consuming.

If, after reading the advice in Chapter 3, you decide to keep to a very strict calorie intake of just 850 to 1,000 calories daily, you will find it very difficult to achieve the upper levels of the fibre recommendation and might even find it difficult to consume 35 grams of fibre daily. Don't worry. In these circumstances 30 grams daily will suffice. You are, you see, still consuming a very high *percentage* of dietary fibre. The average Briton who is not attempting to shed weight is consuming between 2,000 and 3,000 calories daily and only around 15 to 20 grams of fibre. So you will be taking in about twice as much dietary fibre in less than half as much food. You are on a high-fibre diet even on 30 grams a day. So the recommendations are a helpful guide-line, not a biblical edict. No need to get too fussed about the odd gram.

The reasons for increasing your intake of dietary fibre as you cut calories in order to slim are fully explained in *The F-Plan* diet book, and have been overwhelmingly confirmed by the many thousands of people who have shed weight on the F-Plan dieting method. However, for F-Plan beginners here is a summing-up of some of the major advantages of high-fibre dieting.

1. High-fibre foods automatically slow down eating, for several reasons. They require more chewing and swallowing, and also, because of their bulk, provide a greater volume of

food to chew and swallow. Both physically and psychologically this has a most beneficial effect in satisfying the appetite on less food.

2. High-fibre meals are much more filling than other meals. Dietary fibre contains a sponge-like substance which absorbs water and makes food swell to a large volume in the stomach. This remarkable filling effect has been particularly extolled by F-Plan dieters and accounts for the fact that so many who never succeeded in dieting before have succeeded in keeping to the F-Plan method. When the stomach is full you do not feel hungry. When you don't feel hungry you are considerably less susceptible to the food temptations of the Western world. Usually it is the hungry, or at least the semi-hungry person who just simply cannot resist the sight of that tempting food in a shop window and who succumbs to a guilt-ridden binge.

3. High-fibre foods satisfy hunger for longer, because they stay in the stomach for considerably longer than refined carbohydrate foods. Fibre expert Dr Martin Eastwood estimates that while a meal or snack based on refined sugary and starchy foods will usually pass through the stomach in twenty to thirty minutes, a meal containing a high percentage of dietary fibre will stay in the stomach for an hour to an hour and a half. Refined carbohydrate foods, too, because of their chain reaction on the blood sugar level, tend to cause a rebound hunger problem. A couple of hours after eating a meal or snack of this nature you can find yourself feeling more hungry than you were before. Fibre-rich foods, by contrast, do not lead to rebound hunger.

4. High-fibre foods help to speed weight loss because they are less completely digested than other foods. If you are consuming 1,000 calories daily on the F-Plan slimming method, you are actually making appreciably less than 1,000 calories available to the body. The fewer calories your body can use from food, the more it has to withdraw from its own stock of surplus fat, thus more rapidly reducing that bulge on tum or thighs or seat.

One day, perhaps, super scientists will invent the chocolate bar that goes straight through and down the loo . . but that day is still far off. Until it arrives we can at least take comfort in, and advantage from, the fact that a percentage of the calories we are eating in fibre-rich foods like peas, beans, sweetcorn, wholewheat bread and potatoes are costing us nothing in terms of excess poundage and feeding only the bacteria down the sewers.

5. Dietary fibre is a valuable substance in protecting our health. Its manifold advantages in helping to prevent some major diseases of the Western world are becoming increasingly well-known and established.

Many of our major bowel disorders, ranging from cancer of the colon to simple constipation, are virtually unknown in Third World countries, whose inhabitants live on high-fibre diets. Links are being established between the incidence of coronary heart disease and a low intake of dietary fibre, and similarly with the incidence of diabetes.

Research into the medical aspects of dietary fibre is still in its infancy and much more information will undoubtedly be revealed in the coming years. However, enough is already established to have convinced the major medical and nutritional authorities of the Western world that increased dietary fibre intake is of substantial value in preventative medicine.

Perhaps the most convincing factor of all is the current life expectancy of those living in Britain and other Western countries compared with that of high-fibre eaters in Third World countries where infectious diseases are still common, hygiene is poor, medical drugs and aid are sparse and poverty is rife. Once child mortality figures are subtracted, their life expectancy differs little from our own. A rural African who has reached the age of forty has a very similar life expectancy to a British businessman of the same age – and who has begun to approach that period when peculiarly Western diseases, like coronaries and many forms of cancer, become so prevalent.

Medical research into the reasons for these Western killer diseases points to many possible causes inherent in our way of life, but predominant among them are the food substances we are and are not eating. And predominant among those food substances lacking in our diet is sufficient dietary fibre.

There are few, if any, medical and nutritional experts who would argue with the proposition that to increase the dietary fibre content of our meals is a sound and wise precaution to protect health.

While lecturing and broadcasting about the F-Plan throughout the country earlier this year, the author was contacted by many people who revealed that, having been put onto high-fibre diets by their doctors because of bowel disorders, they had been surprised and pleased to find their surplus weight just disappearing – effortlessly and automatically.

So it is possible that some people could shed weight simply by increasing their intake of high-fibre foods. Indeed, this did happen during one scientific experiment when people were simply asked to eat one pound of potatoes (a fibre-rich food) each day and then as much as they liked of anything else.

While this happy result is possible, it is not certain. Nor is it likely that simply by this method slimmers will lose weight at sufficient speed to satisfy their personal goals. For this reason the F-Plan slimming method, which you can follow from the charts in this book, is based on cutting calorie intake as well as increasing intake of dietary fibre.

When you follow the F-Plan you reduce calories, as on any other diet, but you will find it much easier to keep to your calorie quota and will achieve quicker results. That adds up to more weight loss for less willpower.

So read carefully about the other half of the F-Plan formula – the calorie reduction – before embarking on your slimming campaign.

2

How to get the calories right

If you are keeping strictly to 1,000 calories a day and not shedding surplus fat ... then the chances are you are NOT keeping strictly to 1,000 calories a day.

This fact is not intended to hurt anyone's feelings, and still less, dear reader, to cast any aspersions on your honesty and integrity. The truth is that most of us eat (and drink) more calories than we think we are eating (and drinking) in the course of a day. What is more, it is very easy to make mistakes in counting calories. Then there is also that nasty little disorder called 'eating amnesia' which afflicts us all from time to time. Only recently I suffered a modest attack of it myself when recounting what I had eaten, or rather hadn't eaten, that day. 'Mummy,' my son observed after overhearing the conversation, 'if you aren't careful your nose will grow *very*, very long.'

So it is on the basis of us all (EVEN I!) being human and fallible that I have to announce that it is scientifically almost impossible not to shed surplus body fat when calorie intake is strictly limited to 1,000 a day. On the F-Plan it is even less possible – because if you are consuming 1,000 calories a day in the form of fibre-rich meals a percentage of those calories is not digested, as explained in previous chapters. Hence you are providing your body with less than 1,000 calories daily.

My confidence in making the opening statement of this chapter stems not only from scientific fact. Once when I was young, innocent and unaware of eating amnesia, 'weighers-wilt' ('I'll just take a guess at this – looks like two ounces ... !') and other related disorders, I became so alarmed about all the people who couldn't seem to shed weight on 1,000 calories a day that I interviewed many of them, carefully selected a group of twenty of the most baffling and genuine cases, and incarcerated them in a health farm for a week. Then (somewhat sneakily) I had them fed not 1,000 but 1,500 calories daily.

All but two of them shed weight.

The reassuring message from this cautionary tale is that if you are overweight and use the F-Plan calorie chart correctly, as instructed, you simply cannot fail to shed surplus body fat. Health disorders which prevent weight loss are very rare. Almost certainly if you were suffering from such an illness you would have other symptoms to indicate that you were unwell.

The reason why people sometimes think they can't shed weight on a strict calorie ration of 1,000 daily is that they are guessing at the weight – and thus the calorie content – of their portions of food, or forgetting to add in the calories provided by little items like the butter spread on that bread, or the milk in all those cups of tea; or they fail to realize that innocent-looking things like that canned soft drink or glass of orange juice, or the mayonnaise coleslaw served in the office canteen ('Can't contain many calories – it's salad, isn't it!') can add a sizeable number of calories to the daily total.

When people guess at the calorie content of a portion of food they tend to underestimate the calories in meat and cheese, mainly because there was such a deeply entrenched fallacy, persisting for so many years, that 'protein foods' like this could not possibly be fattening. Most people also underestimate the calories provided by fatty foods and fat-containing sauces and dressings. This is simply because the calorie content of these foods is so amazingly high. All fats – butter, margarine, lard, and all the oils including vegetable oils – contain more than 200 calories an ounce. An astronomic figure, when you consider that sugar, for instance, provides, weight for weight, only about half that number of calories, and that potatoes contain only 25 calories an ounce. But again, schooled by the incorrect idea that it is the carbohydrate foods which are the most fattening, many people will very much underestimate the number of calories in the butter-based sauce on their slice of fish, which looks like such an innocent dish.

By the same token, many people *over*estimate the calories provided by potatoes (cooked without fat), cereal foods, and even fat-free sweet foods. Most sweet foods like chocolate, biscuits, cakes and many puddings have a high fat content as well as a high sugar content, so their calorie cost is, indeed, extravagant. However, when sugar is present without much fat or indeed with none, as in a packet of fruit pastilles or some light desserts like crème caramel, the calorie cost is often lower than people imagine.

Of comfort to those of lesser virtue is the fact that pub drinkers, guided only by guesswork, tend to overestimate the calories provided by alcoholic drinks, while innocent orange-juice drinkers, or saintly souls who will 'just stick to a bitter lemon, thanks', often underestimate the number of calories they are consuming. This is based on the deeply entrenched conviction that if it looks naughty it must be very fattening, while if it looks innocent or healthy it cannot be. This is not a totally dependable theory when it comes to calorie counting.

I make the distinction of 'pub drinkers' because home drinkers often pour much larger so-called singles and therefore consume *at least* as many calories as they think they are taking in – frequently even more. This applies to spirits rather than wine, for obvious reasons. And, of course, if the bitter-lemon drinker is insisting on one labelled 'low calorie', he or she is consuming hardly any calories at all and is to be congratulated.

From my own observations, made over many years, another great area of calorie error is cold food. We all associate salads with slimming. So if we are eating, for instance, a slice of calorie-crammed quiche surrounded by salad vegetable concoctions oozing with oily or mayonnaisey dressings we are still eating a salad, aren't we so that can't be very fattening, can it? YES IT CAN Most people very much underestimate the number of calories in cold salad meals served in restaurants, canteens and cafés.

As you will see from all these examples of overestimating and underestimating, guesswork is dangerous, on the whole, when it comes to calorie counting. I use that qualifying phrase 'on the whole' because there are some foods which allow you to get away with it, some meals in restaurants where you can and indeed have to get away with it, and some people who can get away with it. Let us deal with the people first.

The honest truth, never before revealed, is that there are two types of slimmer. One type can get away with near murder, at least for a while, and still shed some weight. The second type cannot get away with anything, and must keep very precisely to a set number of calories, weighing and measuring food carefully, in order to shed weight. Obviously there must be a third type, hovering somewhere in the middle, but you will be able to work this out for yourself by considering the following characteristics of the two extremes.

The CAN-get-away-with-murder calorie counter: This dieter is heavily overweight (by several stones), large in height as well as bulk. He or she has been eating a very large quantity of food and has recently embarked on a calorie-counting slimming programme.

Big people who weigh a lot and eat a lot tend to shed weight very easily and speedily when they start cutting down on calorie intake. So even if they are inadvertently or wilfully slipping down a couple of hundred more calories than they intend in the course of a day, they might still find themselves clocking up a decent weight loss on the scales each week.

My message to them: Good luck, and as long as you are satisfied with your weekly weight loss by all means continue to do your own thing. But do be aware that being a little easy-going in working out and rationing your calories can easily allow you to drift down the slippery slope towards being *too* easy-going to achieve weight loss. Such is the frailty of most of our natures that once we take a toe off the straight and narrow we tend to slide off it altogether.

Also, be aware that this happy state of reward for only relative virtue will not continue indefinitely. The body adjusts to lower calorie intake during prolonged periods of dieting, with the result that weight loss tends to slow down. This means that, as we continue to diet, we must reduce calorie intake a little more in order to go on achieving a satisfactory rate of weight loss. This in turn means being even more strict and exact in measuring out the food and counting up the calories. So if your regular weigh-ins start to yield disappointing news, you know what to do.

The C A N 'T-get-away-with-anything (darn it!) calorie counter: If you belong to this category you are probably a little person. Things are very unfairly stacked against the short when it comes to slimming. Not only do we display even two or three surplus pounds in the form of an enormous bulge – tall people can often carry a surplus stone without showing it – but we also tend to burn up fewer calories than people of larger height and frame. That means we have to eat less than they do in order to shed weight.

Being only 5′ 2½″ tall myself I too feel very strongly about the unfairness of this, but there is absolutely nothing I can do about it except to warn you that in these circumstances you do need to be very accurate in counting calories in order to achieve a good rate of weight loss. The same applies to anyone, tall or short, who has been dieting for a lengthy period already, and generally to those who are only a few pounds overweight. Weigh, rather than guess, is the general rule to follow in this situation.

Those referred to at the beginning of this chapter, the dieters who think they can't shed weight on 1,000 calories a day, almost invariably belong to the can't-get-away-with-anything group and are not following the essential rules of calorie counting sufficiently strictly So this is a timely moment to list those rules Even if you belong to the getting-

away-with-murder group, the time will come when you have
to follow the rules precisely in order to maintain a speedy
weight loss. So here we go:

1. *Be aware that ALL foods, not just some foods, supply
calories.* Every single food you see in every supermarket,
butcher's, greengrocer's and fishmonger's in the land has
calories lurking within. Fibre-rich foods provide calories,
too. Because this book explains the many ways in which
fibre-rich foods help you to shed weight, I don't want you
to imagine that they are calorie-free. In the bad old days of
low-carbohydrate diets, many people did, indeed, imagine
that those saintly 'protein foods' were calorie-free – I have
even known poor souls pouring down vastly fattening cream
under the mistaken impression that it was calorie-free because it lacked carbohydrate! Let no similar mistake arise
with the F-Plan. The foods which supply you with fibre
also supply you with calories. Some of those calories are,
in fact, wasted and won't add to your weight. But as we
don't yet know how many are wasted, be on the safe side:
count the full number given in the F-Plan Calorie and Fibre
Charts, and reap the advantage in speed of weight loss.

2. *Weigh your food.* Calories are worked out on a per
ounce basis (or in grams, for the modern metric-minded),
so how many calories you eat in a portion of food depends
on the weight of the portion of food you are eating, WEIGH
IT is the key phrase for the calorie-counter. Not weighing it
is the key crime. It simply isn't possible to follow a calorie-
counting method of slimming without owning some dependably accurate weighing scales – ideally, dietary scales,
because with some foods like fats you need to weigh out
very small portions.

Most diet advisers sternly insist that you weigh every
single thing before putting it in your mouth (cigarettes and
fingernails, only, excluded). My own attitude, stemming
from a kindly nature, is more permissive. Frankly I think
you would look pretty silly weighing out your lettuce when
an ounce provides only THREE calories. So what if you go

berserk and eat an ounce more lettuce than you think you are eating! Let us be adult about this and accept that, in view of the fact that even the very strictest diets suggest that you eat not much less than 1,000 calories daily, those *three* calories aren't going to make a jot of difference to your weight loss.

On the other hand – and this is where many people go wrong – that tiny bit of butter that you sneak onto a crispbread IS going to make a difference because there are such an enormous number of calories in such a very modest quantity of fat. The best tip in using fats like butter, margarine or their lower-calorie alternatives such as Outline or St Ivel Gold is to weigh out half an ounce or an ounce each morning and make that your ready-calorie-counted ration for the day—saves a lot of fiddling around with small quantities. Ditto for the milk you are going to use throughout the day in all those cups of tea and coffee. However, I digress . . .

Earlier in this chapter I explained that with some foods you CAN get away with guesswork about quantity, and weighing is unnecessary. These foods are low-calorie vegetables and just a few low-calorie fruits, and we discuss them in Chapter 4. Apart from these, weigh all foods you eat when using the F-plan Calorie and Fibre Chart.

Also listed in Chapter 4 are the meals you can calorie count by guesswork when eating out in restaurants.

3. *Remember that many drinks supply calories, too.* These are every bit as fattening as the calories in solid food, and must be taken into account in reaching your daily total calorie intake. Happily, many drinks are calorie-free or near enough not to matter, and you can drink as much as you like of these. Again, they are listed in Chapter 4.

Earlier in this chapter I explained that it is nearly impossible not to shed surplus weight on a total calorie intake of 1,000 a day when you are following the F-Plan method. I cited that 1,000-calorie total because, to my knowledge, all adults in normal health and circumstances burn up *more* than 1,000 calories daily. Shedding surplus weight depends on providing your body with fewer calories than it needs to keep going. This is the only way in which it can be forced to feed on its own surplus fat. Never believe anything else, whatever silly things you may read or hear elsewhere.

Different bodies have differing calorie requirements to function and fuel their energy output. Size, in both height and weight, is a major factor, and this largely explains why men use more calories than women. The latest scientific investigations into how many calories the average Briton is burning up in this modern labour-saving, sedentary age are yielding somewhat depressing indications.

At one time I would have suggested that everyone would shed surplus fat on a ration of 1,500 calories daily. However, some of my medical and scientific friends now suspect that some women burn up only 1,500 calories daily – so obviously, on this intake, they would maintain weight rather than reduce surplus fat.

However, I am not personally aware of any research revealing that adult British people of either sex or any size can live on 1,000 calories daily without shedding weight, whether they are aiming to do so or not. For this reason 1,000 calories daily is a pretty safe, 'can't fail' figure.

This does not mean, though, that it is the ideal daily calorie quota for every F-Plan dieter. In the next chapter you will find guidance on your own ideal daily calorie ration.

3

How many calories?

In order to shed surplus body fat it is necessary for an adult to ration calories to between 1,000 and 1,500 daily. In *The F-Plan* diet book I recommend 1,000 calories as the absolute minimum on the sound basis that the F-Plan slimming diet is designed to improve rather than endanger your health. The method ensures a healthy intake of dietary fibre, but minerals, vitamins and protein are important – and on too modest a total daily ration of food you run more risk of going short of these.

You will appreciate that, as well as worrying about your health, I have my own reputation to worry about! Diet authors who write odd things about pineapples and suchlike get a fearsome tongue-lashing from members of the medical profession – thoroughly deserved, in my view. The same goes for any diet authors who recommend slimming methods which might leave you short of essential nutrients.

So far, after more than fifteen years of advising on diets, I have managed to maintain a reputation, in the eyes of leaders of the medical profession and of specialists in nutrition, for being really quite sane, sound and sensible. And you will quite see that I do not want to find angry battalions of professors, doctors and nutritionists suddenly besieging me with cross phone calls and furious letters, and setting up bonfires in order to burn my book in their universities and hospitals.

I venture to bore you with my personal anxieties merely because of a question which has cropped up frequently since *The F-Plan* was first published. Probably because the fibre-rich food is so filling, many people ask: Do I HAVE to eat a thousand calories a day if I can manage with less?

I have given much thought to this (despite an implication in the *Sunday Times* I do *not* spend all my time sitting thinking on the loo – but this is, indeed, a peaceful place for contemplation, isn't it?). The answer: Oh, all right – reduce calorie intake to 850 if you must, but ONLY in these circumstances:

1. *If you are just thinking in terms of an occasional day, maybe a couple of days a week.* Our desire for food tends to vary from day to day. On some days it is easy to eat very little, on others it is difficult to keep to even the most generous diet. It seems sensible to take advantage of the good days in order to make allowance for any excess eating on the difficult days, and dieting calorie intake can be averaged out on a weekly basis. If you eat more on some days and less on others, you will shed weight just as successfully as if you stuck to the same number of calories each day.

2. *If you are only planning to follow the F-Plan for a week or two to polish off a modest weight problem of just a few pounds.* If you have been following a normal varied British pattern of eating you have probably been consuming less dietary fibre than you need for health protection, but it is unlikely that you are deficient in minerals and vitamins. In those circumstances, vitamin and mineral deficiencies do not crop up in a couple of weeks. However, on a calorie intake of below 1,000 a day it is a reasonable idea to take a multi-vitamin pill with iron – just to keep your mother, and me, happy.

Frankly, the only people I can think of who need to go as low as 850 calories a day in order to achieve a pacey weight loss on the F-Plan are small, rather sedentary women, only a few pounds overweight, and those struggling off the last few pounds of excess weight after a prolonged dieting campaign. In these circumstances, increasing energy expenditure helps, too – by which I mean generally moving around as much as possible, doing a lot of brisk walking and speeding this up to running pace if you are young. Swimming, as long as you really do swim from end to end of the pool repeatedly rather than dallying about in the shallow end chatting with a friend, is an excellent method of burning up calories and firming up your muscles.

In answer to another common question from those about to embark on the F-Plan: No, it is not necessary to exercise in order to shed weight. The F-Plan method can make you slim without additional exercises. However, having said that, I am very strongly in favour of increasing physical activity and am among those who suspect that its value in weight control has been much underestimated.

In my experience, the major mistake that dieters make lies in deciding that they *will* exercise once they get slim, rather than starting to increase their physical activity as they start to diet. We had a typical example of this during the F-Plan trials at London University. One attractive but heavily overweight young lady revealed that she spent most of her evenings sitting chatting to friends in a wine bar while dieting. She *did* intend to join a nearby sports club, where she could swim regularly, as soon as she was slim, but meanwhile she shyly admitted to feeling too embarrassed to be seen in a swimsuit.

The situation arising from this all-too-common attitude was as follows: in the evening she was placing herself in a situation of maximum temptation as far as diet-breaking was concerned – with time on her hands and food and drink all too readily available. There is nothing quite as bad as watching other people eat and drink what you are trying to avoid. Had she embarked on an evening swim instead, she would have achieved all these advantages in helping her to keep to her diet:

1. She would have been kept busy and occupied, and well away from the sight, smell and temptation of food.
2. She would have experienced the undoubted lift in spirits that results from physical exercise. Depressed moods are the most difficult moods for dieting, and such is the

mood-lifting effect of exercise that it is even being used medically as part of the treatment for depression.

3. She would have burned up extra calories, thus helping to speed her weight loss still more.

4. She would have experienced that glow of virtue which is so conducive to easy dieting. When we feel pleased with our achievements we tend to feel inspired to achieve even more in the way of health and figure improvement.

I am very well aware of the sensitivity of anyone who is overweight. It can often arise even when people are a mere few pounds overweight. But if you are contemplating increasing physical activity for still further benefit to your health and figure, try to realize that those vast crowds of people who will scream with laughter at the sight of you in a swimsuit, or on seeing you jogging, skipping, enrolling at aerobics classes or even taking a brisk daily walk, exist only in your mind. The best time to start exercising is at the start rather than at the end of a dieting campaign.

But back to calories. Here is a guide to your ideal daily calorie intake when you are shedding weight with the aid of The F-Plan Calorie and Fibre Chart.

Allow yourself 1,500 calories daily
● If you are male, of at least medium height, and more than half a stone overweight;
● If you are female, more than two stones overweight, and just embarking on a weight-loss programme as opposed to switching from some other slimming diet on which you have already lost some of your surplus weight.

Allow yourself 1,000 calories daily
● If you are a small man with only a few pounds of surplus weight;
● If you are female and less than one stone overweight;
● If you are female and more than a stone overweight, but have already been dieting and have lost a stone or more by another slimming method.

Allow yourself 850 calories daily
● ONLY in the circumstances described earlier in this chapter.

Of course you may choose to set your daily calorie intake at between 1,000 and 1,500. There are a few people who would not shed weight on the F-Plan on 1,250 calories daily, which can prove a comfortable yet quick weight-shedding level. You will find a full explanation of the many factors which affect individual rates of weight loss and an ideal dieting calorie intake in this book's partner publication, *The F-Plan* diet book.

4

OK – don't weigh!

This is the permissive chapter of this book. In it we discuss the drinks you can drink with freedom, the foods which don't have to be weighed, and the restaurant dishes at which you can take an educated guess, when you diet with the F-Plan Calorie and Fibre Chart.

Calorie-free drinks

The fact that calorie-free liquids don't add to your weight or prevent you from shedding those surplus pounds has been emphasized so often that I feel deeply embarrassed at having to state it again. Yet write it I must. The fallacy of 'fluid retention' has almost become part of our folklore.

If the body did not possess a very precise mechanism for controlling its fluid content and expelling surplus liquid consumed, people would go round bursting and exploding all over the place. Drinks parties would become absolutely hazardous unless one went in waterproofs and wellies.

Seriously, there are some medical drugs which appear to raise the fluid level of the body a little; and there are minor fluid fluctuations of just a few pounds which can account for those swollen ankles or that bloated feeling before the monthly period. But, apart from these minor and temporary fluctuations, fluid retention is not the cause of weight problems. There is no point in cutting down on fluid intake while dieting. On the F-Plan diet method it is, in fact, a good idea to drink a generous quantity of calorie-free fluid.

The calorie-supplying drinks are listed in the Drinks Calorie Chart starting on page 121. Obviously, the calories supplied by these drinks have to be included in your daily dieting total. Below is a list of drinks which can be consumed absolutely freely because the calories they supply, if any, are too few to be worth counting.

Water – of course. This includes the fizzy waters, like Perrier, which people have taken to buying in bottles.

Tea and coffee. As a matter of fact, caffeine, which is present in both these drinks, has a modest effect in speeding metabolism – the rate at which you burn calories. So not only are tea and coffee not fattening, they could actually be said to be 'slimming' to a small degree. Of course, what goes into tea and coffee can be fattening. A slice of lemon in tea, or saccharin in either drink, adds no calories. Milk does add calories (much less so if it is skimmed milk) and so does sugar; these must be included in the daily calorie total.

Drinks labelled 'low-calorie'. This is a dependable label, which virtually means no calories. Certainly too few to be worth bothering about. These days many manufacturers of canned and bottled drinks make a low-calorie range. These include Canada Dry mixers, Energen one-calorie drinks, Hunt's low-calorie mixers, Schweppes Slimline range, and Chekwate, Concorde, Safeway, Sunfresh, Tesco and Waitrose low-calorie drinks. From the cola manufacturers there is Diet Pepsi and Tab.

Bovril and Oxo. These do supply a few calories, but too few to be worth counting, and can provide a nice, hot, comforting drink on a dieting evening.

Lemon juice. Unlike other fruit juices, lemon juice is virtually calorie-free, as it lacks the sugar present in the juice of other fruit. Obviously you would need to sweeten this unless you have very eccentric taste buds – but saccharin sweeteners can do the job without calorie cost.

Guessable foods

Quite a large number of vegetables – the leafy green ones, in particular – provide only a tiny number of calories and are eaten only in modest quantity in terms of weight. An average serving of lettuce, for instance, weighs only about an ounce and that provides just three calories. With watercress your portion would probably only weigh half an ounce, amounting to a massive two calories! Were you to become an utter glutton and pile your plate with a mountain of watercress you would still be able to count the calories on the fingers of your hands. From which you will see that it simply isn't worth the bother of weighing some foods when you are counting calories.

Which foods these are will become clearly evident when you look through the Instant Calorie and Fibre Chart, showing average portions, which starts on page 57. I suggest that where an average portion provides less than 20 calories you let yourself off the chore of weighing while following the F-Plan slimming method.

Sometimes the vegetables which are particularly low in calories are not particularly high in fibre. This means they don't do you much good, but neither do they do you any harm. Some vegetables, like cucumber, radishes and lettuce, are mainly water with the occasional vitamin floating around here and there.

Dieters have asked whether they can add these low-calorie vegetables to the meals in *The F-Plan* book, and the answer is: Yes. Eat the high-fibre vegetables for their value in health and weight control, but by all means add more variety and colour to your plate, if you wish, with these harmless foods which don't provide enough calories to slow your weight loss.

Discussion of these vegetables provides me with my chance to make a suitable riposte to the lady who wrote to a national newspaper drawing attention to such ungainly 'F-Plan dieters' as the rhino and warthog. True, madam, the figures of these creatures leave something to be desired in aesthetic terms. But the digestive and food utilization processes of such ruminants are vastly different from our own, which is why we can't simply put the family out to graze in a meadow rather than spend a fortune at Tesco.

If you must conjure up some inspirational animal image

as you adjust your menus towards a little more plant food and a little less animal food, may I commend the gazelle

Eating out

As I explain in *The F-Plan* diet book, seeking dietary fibre in most restaurant meals is a fairly futile task. Since writing it, I have made one personal step forward by making a practice of ordering baked potatoes and discovering, rather to my surprise, that you really can come to enjoy and prefer them without butter or cream. For those who don't share my acquired taste, *The F-Plan* diet book gives recipes for some low-calorie dressings for potatoes baked at home.

On the whole, however, those dining or lunching out from time to time while dieting with the F-Plan Calorie and Fibre Chart would be wise to concentrate on choosing only very simple, dependably low-calorie dishes. Here is a small eating-out calorie chart of safe guesses. Safe, because where there is likely to be any significant variation I have ruthlessly estimated the maximum figure.

Calorie Guide to Restaurant Dishes

Dish	Maximum calorie total per serving
Starters	
Consommé	60
Grapefruit, half a fresh fruit	20
Melon, generous slice	40
Fresh fruit cocktail	60
Oysters, each	5
Smoked salmon	80
Parma ham with melon (don't eat the ham fat)	150
Main courses	
Grilled Dover sole (not buttery)	350
Grilled liver	250
Lobster, plain boiled or grilled	200
Steak, medium to well grilled (6oz)	300
Seafood – crab, prawns, etc. – minus mayonnaise or any other form of added fat	100
Omelette (not cheese)	350
Desserts	
Fruit sorbet	100
Crème caramel	200
Ice cream (plain ice without added cream, etc.)	150

Average portions of fresh fruits and vegetables and other simple restaurant foods can be seen on our Instant Calorie and Fibre Guide, starting on page 57.

5

The F-Plan dieting rules and recommendations

Here are the essential rules to follow in order to devise your own highly effective weight-shedding menus from the F-Plan charts in this book.

1. Ensure that the sum total of all the calories you eat and drink in a day does not exceed your ideal dieting intake. This could range from 850 to 1,500 calories daily, and you will find guidance on your own intake in Chapter 3.

2. Choose your foods from the charts to ensure a daily intake of more than 30g of dietary fibre. Between 35g and 50g is the F-Plan recommendation, but this could be lowered a little by those on very low-calorie, short-term slimming programmes.

3. To get maximum benefit in making your diet easy, speedy and healthy, obtain your dietary fibre from a wide range of cereal, fruit and vegetable foods – rather than seeking to make up the total from just one or two very fibre-rich foods.

4. If you are planning to diet for more than two or three weeks it is recommended that you have half a pint of *skimmed* milk (100 calories) daily as a nutritional precaution.

Making it really easy
To make it really easy to reach your daily dietary fibre target of 30g plus, it is an excellent idea to have one regular, constant daily meal – breakfast is ideal because we tend not to vary our breakfasts – to supply about half the requirement. Add a couple of pieces of fruit each day as part of

your menu, and after that it isn't at all difficult to include enough dietary fibre in your other two meals to succeed in your aims.

One of the great successes of the F-Plan method has been such a meal, a kind of home-made muesli, called Fibre-Filler. Dieters found this enormously filling, and not surprisingly, because it supplies a full 15g of dietary fibre from nicely varied sources. The recipe is included at the end of this chapter.

Ready packaged foods can help to provide an alternative. One of the remarkable effects of the F-Plan diet is the major influence it has already had on the sales pattern of foods in Britain, signalling a major upswing in the consumption of foods like wholewheat and granary bread, bran, and bran cereals.

Britain is at last beginning to eat in the way that our medical and nutritional advisers have been urging us to eat – and, quick to spot the trend, manufacturers already have new fibre-rich foods in the pipeline which are likely to appear in the shops later this year. So, with the aid of these and the fibre figures revealed for the first time in this book, it becomes easier and easier to shed weight and improve health with the F-Plan.

For F-Plan beginners, aiming to plan their own menus from the calorie and fibre figures in these charts, the ready calorie- and fibre-counted meals in *The F-Plan* diet book will also be of great help. There are about two hundred of these – meals on wholewheat toast or pasta, jacket potato meals, high-fibre salads, meals making use of high-fibre foods like baked beans, peas, spinach. They give you lots of ideas and put you on the right track in switching to this new, better way of eating.

Here is the recipe for Fibre-Filler. The quantities below, suggested for one day's portion, provide you with 200 calories and 15g of dietary fibre from nicely varied sources. When you include this as part of your regular daily dieting pattern it obviously makes sense to make up several portions at one time and store in a jar in separate ready-measured daily portion bags.

For one day (200 calories, 15g fibre)
½oz (14g) Bran Flakes
½oz (14g) bran
½oz (14g) All Bran or Bran Buds
¼oz (7g) almonds, chopped
¼oz (7g) dried prune (just one large fruit), stoned and chopped
¼oz (7g) dried apricots, chopped
½oz (14g) sultanas

Instant Calorie and Fibre Guide and Chart

Instant Calorie and Fibre Guide

Is it very fattening? Is it rich in fibre? Because this chart gives the calorie and dietary fibre contents of average or easily recognizable portions of all the basic foods, it provides an instant answer to these questions.

Few of us can picture an ounce of lamb chop or an ounce of apple, pear or peach, but we do get a clear picture of an average-sized whole loin chop, or an apple, pear or peach. Are these foods costing us much in calories and what, if anything, is each one contributing to our intake of dietary fibre? The answers emerge clearly here, as do the foods which will be of greatest value in boosting our fibre intake as we follow the F-Plan method of dieting.

Only foods which are most easily recognizable on a 'per ounce' basis are listed in that form in this chart. However, as you measure your food to keep within your calorie total, your portion or piece of a particular food may be larger or smaller than the average one itemized here. For this reason we also provide a Basic Calorie and Fibre Chart, starting on page 127, which reveals the calories and dietary fibre in a single ounce of each of the foods listed here.

Use the Instant Calorie and Fibre Chart to check which foods are low enough in calories to help you keep within your total and high enough in fibre to help you to reach that daily target.

Use the Basic Calorie and Fibre Chart for measuring and calculating.

Use the ready-planned low-calorie high-fibre meals in *The F-Plan* diet book, and the additional section at the end of this book, when you prefer your meals to be worked out for you. Most people will find that a combination of ready-planned meals with some meals they plan themselves will provide them with the easiest and most flexible formula

In this guide we list only very basic packaged foods like cornflakes. But these days, with a growing awareness of the value of dietary fibre for health and weight control, many manufacturers are packaging useful fibre-rich foods. Some other canned, frozen and packaged foods just happen to be useful sources of dietary fibre because of the nature of their contents. You will find our valuable Calorie and Fibre Guide to Packaged Foods on page 85.

In this chart, calorie figures are rounded off to the nearest 5, and fibre figures to the nearest half gram, for easy calculation. Dietary fibre figures should always be considered as an approximate rather than a precise guide. The figures we give are sufficiently dependable to take your daily intake up to the right level to help reduce your weight and protect your health.

Instant Calorie and Fibre Chart

Food	Portion	Calories	Fibre g
All Bran	1½oz (42g), average breakfast bowl	105	11·5
Almonds	1 shelled almond	10	0·5
ground	1 level tablespoon (15ml)	30	1·0
Apples			
eating	5oz (142g), average-sized fruit	50	2·0
cooking			
baked	8oz (227g), average-sized baking apple	70	4·5
stewed without sugar	6oz (170g)	55	3·5
Apricots			
fresh			
weighed with stone	1oz (28g), average-sized fruit	5	0·5
stoned and stewed without sugar	6oz (170g)	40	3·0
dried, stewed without sugar	4oz (113g) cooked weight	75	10.0
canned	4oz (113g), fruit and syrup	120	1.5

Food	Portion	Calories	Fibre g
Arrowroot	1 level teaspoon (5ml)	10	0
Asparagus, boiled	1 spear	5	0·5
Aubergines, raw, flesh only	1 aubergine, 7oz (200g)	30	5·0
Avocado, flesh only	½ avocado, 3½oz (99g)	215	2.0
Bacon	1 bacon steak, grilled, 3½oz (99g) raw weight	105	0
	1 back rasher		
	raw	150	0
	grilled	85	0
	fried	95	0
	1 streaky rasher		
	raw	85	0
	grilled	60	0
	fried	70	0
Banana	6oz (110g), average-sized fruit	80	3·5
Barcelona nuts, shelled	1oz (28g)	180	3·0

	½oz (14g) raw weight, amount in average portion of thick broth	50	1·0
Barley, pearl			
Bean sprouts			
raw	2oz (56g), average salad portion	15	0·5
cooked	2oz (56g)	20	0·5
Beans			
adzuki, uncooked	1oz (28g) dry weight	90	7·0
baked, canned in tomato sauce	8oz (227g), one small can	145	16·5
black-eyed, uncooked	1oz (28g) dry weight	95	7·0
broad, boiled	4oz (113g)	50	5·0
butter, canned	4oz (113g) drained weight	110	5·5
french, boiled	4oz (113g)	10	3·5
haricot, uncooked	1oz (28g) dry weight	75	7·0
red kidney			
uncooked	1oz (28g) dry weight, usual portion in a dish like chilli con carne	75	7·0
boiled	3oz (85g), average portion in salad	75	7·0
canned	3oz (85g) drained weight, average portion in a dish like chilli con carne	75	7·0
runner, boiled	4oz (113g)	20	4·0
soya, uncooked	1oz (28g) dry weight	110	4·0

Food	Portion	Calories	Fibre g
Beef			
beefburgers, frozen	average 2oz (56g) beefburger		
	grilled	130	0
	well grilled	85	0
brisket, boiled	3oz (85g)	275	0
corned, canned	2oz (56g)	120	0
forerib, roast	3oz (85g), lean only	190	0
mince, stewed	3oz (85g)	180	0
rump steak, grilled	4oz (113g), lean only	190	0
silverside, salted, boiled	3oz (85g), lean only	145	0
sirloin, roast	3oz (85g), lean only	160	0
stewing steak, stewed	3oz (85g)	185	0
topside, roast	3oz (85g), lean only	130	0
Beef sausages	1 large sausage, grilled	130	0
	1 small sausage (chipolata), grilled	60	0
Beef and pork sausages	1 large sausage, grilled	135	0
	1 small sausage (chipolata), grilled	65	0
Beetroot, boiled	2oz (56g)	25	1·5
Bemax (wheatgerm)	¼oz (7g), 1 level tablespoon (15ml)	25	0·5

Biscuits, *see* Packaged Food Chart			
Black pudding, fried	2oz (56g)	170	0·5
Blackberries, stewed without sugar	4oz (113g)	30	7·0
Blackcurrants, stewed without sugar	4oz (113g)	30	8·5
Bran	¼oz (7g), 2½ level tablespoons (37ml)	15	3·0
Brawn	2oz (56g)	85	0
Brazil nuts	1 shelled brazil nut	20	0·5
Bread (*see also* p. 91 for individual manufacturers' breads)			
brown	2½oz (70g), two average slices	155	3·5
wheatgerm (e.g. Hovis)	2oz (56g), two average slices	130	2·5
white	2½oz (70g), two average slices	160	2·0
wholemeal	2½oz (70g), two average slices	150	6·0

Food	Portion	Calories	Fibre g
Bread rolls			
brown			
crusty	2oz (56g), average size	160	3·5
soft	2oz (56g), average size	170	3·0
white			
crusty	2oz (56g), average size	160	2·0
soft	2oz (56g), average size	170	1·5
wholemeal (e.g. Allinson)	1½oz (42g), average size	90	3·5
Broccoli tops, boiled	4oz (113g)	20	4·5
Brussels sprouts, boiled	4oz (113g)	20	3·0
Butter	½oz (14g), average daily allowance on a calorie-controlled diet	105	0
Cabbage			
red, raw	1oz (28g), average serving of pickled cabbage	5	1·0
savoy, boiled	4oz (113g)	10	3·0
spring, boiled	4oz (113g)	10	2·5
white, raw	3oz (85g), average portion in coleslaw	20	2·5
winter, boiled	4oz (113g)	15	3·0

Food	Description	Calories	Fibre
Cake			
fruit			
plain	2oz (56g), average slice	200	1·5
rich, iced	1oz (28g), 1 small slice	100	1·0
sponge, with fat, jam-filled	2oz (56g), 1 average slice	170	0·5
Carrots			
raw	2oz (56g), 1 medium-sized whole carrot	10	1·5
boiled	4oz (113g)	20	3·5
canned	4oz (113g) drained weight	20	4·0
Cashew nuts	1oz (28g)	150	0·5
Cauliflower			
raw	2oz (56g), average amount in a salad	10	1·0
boiled	4oz (113g)	10	2·0
Celeriac, boiled	4oz (113g)	15	5·5
Celery			
raw	2oz (56g), 1 large stick	5	1·0
boiled	4oz (113g)	5	2·5
Cherries			
eating	4oz (113g)	45	1·5
glacé	1 cherry	10	0

Food	Portion	Calories	Fibre g
Chestnuts, shelled	1oz (28g)	50	2·0
Chicken roast drumstick, grilled	3oz (85g), meat only, no skin 3½oz (99g) weight before cooking	125 90	0 0
Chicken joint, baked or grilled	8oz (227g) weight before cooking	180	0
Chicory, raw	1oz (28g), salad serving	3	0·5
Chinese leaves, raw	2oz (56g), salad serving	5	1·0
Chips, fried in deep fat	4oz (113g), small portion	280	2·0
Chocolate, drinking	2 rounded teaspoons (20ml)	40	0
Christmas pudding	2oz (56g), small portion	170	1·0
Cocoa powder	1 rounded teaspoon (10ml)	20	0
Coconut, fresh	1oz (28g)	100	4·0
Cod fillet, fresh, steamed or poached steak, frozen, raw	6oz (170g) weight before cooking 4oz (113g)	125 80	0 0

Coffee, instant, powder or granules	1 rounded teaspoon (10ml)	0	0
Coffee and chicory essence	1 teaspoon (5ml)	10	0
Coley, raw	6oz (170g)	120	0
Condensed milk, whole, sweetened	1 tablespoon (15ml)	50	0
Corn oil	1 tablespoon (15ml)	125	0
Corned beef	2oz (56g)	120	0
Cornflakes	1oz (28g), average breakfast bowl	105	3·0
Cornflour	1 level tablespoon (15ml)	35	0·5
Cottage cheese	4oz (113g) carton	110	0
Crab, canned	1½oz (42g) can	60	0
Cream	1 tablespoon (15ml) double	60	0
	1 tablespoon (15ml) single	30	0
Crispbreads, see p. 90 for individual manufacturers' crispbreads			
Crisps, potato	0.88oz (25g), 1 small packet	130	3·0

Food	Portion	Calories	Fibre g
Cucumber	2oz (56g), salad serving	5	0
Currants, dried	½oz (14g)	35	1·0
Custard powder	1 level tablespoon (15ml)	35	0·5
Damsons, stewed without sugar	4oz (113g)	30	3·5
Dates, dried, stoneless	2oz (56g)	140	5·0
Egg, whole, raw, boiled or poached in water	size 1	95	0
	size 2	90	0
	size 3	80	0
	size 4	75	0
	size 5	70	0
	size 6	60	0
Egg white	1 white of size 3 egg	15	0
Egg yolk	1 yolk of size 3 egg	65	0
Eggplant, *see* **Aubergines**			

Endive, raw	2 oz (56g), salad serving	5	1·0
Evaporated milk, whole	1 tablespoon (15ml)	25	0
Figs			
fresh, raw	1oz (28g), average-sized fruit	10	0·5
dried	2oz (56g) dry weight, about three dried figs	120	10·5
dried, stewed without sugar	4oz (113g)	130	11·5
Fish fingers, frozen	1 fish finger, grilled without fat	50	0
Flour, see Your Basic Calorie and Fibre Chart			
Fruit salad, canned	4oz (113g) fruit and juice	110	1·0
Glacé cherries, see under Cherries			
Golden syrup	1 tablespoon (15ml)	60	0
Goose, roast	3oz (85g), meat only	265	0
Gooseberries			
ripe, raw	2oz (56g)	20	2·0
stewed without sugar	4oz (113g)	15	3·0

Food	Portion	Calories	Fibre g
Grapefruit			
whole	5oz (142g), half average-sized fruit	15	0·5
canned in natural juice	4oz (113g)	45	0·5
Grapenuts	1½oz (42g), average breakfast bowl	150	3·0
Grapes			
black	4oz (113g)	55	0·5
white (green)	4oz (113g)	70	1·0
Greengages, stewed without			
sugar	4oz (113g)	45	2·5
Guavas, canned	4oz (113g)	70	4·0
Haddock			
fillets, fresh	6oz (170g) raw weight	120	0
smoked, steamed	6oz (170g) cooked weight	170	0
Ham			
boiled	2oz (56g), lean only	95	0
cooked and vacuum-packed	2oz (56g), 2–3 slices	80	0
canned	3oz (85g), salad serving	100	0

		105	1·5
Hazelnuts	1oz (28g) shelled weight		
Heart, lamb's, roast	4oz (113g), average-sized heart	270	0
Herring, grilled	5oz (142g), whole herring weighed raw after head and bones removed	280	0
Honey	1 level teaspoon (5ml)	15	0
Ice cream	2oz (56g)	95	0
Jam	1 level teaspoon (5ml)	15	0
Jelly, made up with water	4oz (113g)	70	0
Kidney			
lamb	2oz (56g), average raw weight	50	0
ox	2oz (56g), average portion in a steak-and-kidney casserole	50	0
Kipper, grilled	6oz (170g), whole kipper weighed before cooking	280	0

Food	Portion	Calories	Fibre g
Lamb			
breast, roast	4oz (113g), lean and fat, no bone	460	0
leg, roast	3oz (85g), lean only	162	0
loin chops, grilled	5oz (142g), average-sized chop, raw weight	310	0
shoulder, roast	3oz (85g), lean only	165	0
Lard	½oz (14g)	125	0
Leeks, boiled	4oz (113g)	30	4·5
Lemon sole, fried coated in crumbs	4oz (113g), average-sized fish	190	0·5
Lentils, uncooked	1½oz (42g), in portion of soup	125	5·0
Lettuce, raw	1oz (28g), salad serving	5	0·5
Liver			
calf	4oz (113g) raw weight, average serving for grilling	170	0
chicken	2oz (56g) raw weights, average amount in chicken liver pâté or for fried livers on toast	75	0

Food	Measure	Calories	Fibre
lamb	4oz (113g) raw weight, average casserole serving	200	0
Liver sausage	1oz (28g), sufficient for one round of sandwiches	85	0
Loganberries stewed without sugar	4oz (113g)	15	6·5
canned in syrup	4oz (113g), fruit and syrup	110	3·5
Low-fat spread (e.g. Outline, St Ivel Gold)	1oz (28g), average daily allowance in a calorie-controlled diet	105	0
Luncheon meat, canned	2oz (56g)	175	0
Lychees, canned	4oz (113g), fruit and syrup	75	0·5
Macaroni, wholewheat	2oz (56g) dry weight	195	5·5
Mackerel whole, raw	8oz (227g)	320	0
smoked	6oz (170g)	420	0
Mandarin oranges, canned in syrup	4oz (113g), fruit and syrup	65	0·5

Food	Portion	Calories	Fibre g
Mangoes, canned	4oz (113g), fruit and syrup	90	1·0
Margarine, all brands	½oz (14g), usual daily allowance in a calorie-controlled diet	105	0
Marmalade	1 level teaspoon (5ml)	15	0
Marrow, boiled	4oz (113g)	10	1·0
Marzipan	½oz (14g)	60	1·0
Mayonnaise	1 tablespoon (15ml)	95	0
Melon			
cantaloup, honeydew or yellow	8oz (227g), average slice with skin	30	1·0
ogen	12oz (340g), average whole melon	60	2·5
water	8oz (227g), average slice with skin	25	1·0
Milk, dried, skimmed	1 rounded teaspoon (10ml), average serving in tea or coffee	10	0
Mincemeat	½oz (14g), average weight in a mince pie	35	0·5
Muesli	2oz (56g), average breakfast bowl	205	4·0

Mulberries	4oz (113g) raw weight	40	2·0
Mushrooms	4oz (113g) raw weight	15	3·0
Mustard and cress	¼oz (7g), salad or sandwich serving	1	0
Nectarines	5oz (142g), average-sized whole fruit	65	3·0
Oatcakes	1oz (28g)	125	1·0
Oatmeal	1oz (28g) raw weight, to make average bowl of porridge	110	2·0
Olive oil	1 tablespoon (15ml)	125	0
Onion boiled raw	4oz (113g) ½oz (14g), salad serving	15 5	1·5 0
Orange, whole	6oz (170g), average-sized fruit	40	2·5
Parsley	½oz (14g)	5	1·5
Parsnips, boiled	4oz (113g)	65	3·0

Food	Portion	Calories	Fibre g
Passion fruit, raw	3oz (85g), average-sized fruit	10	5·5
Pawpaw, canned	4oz (113g)	70	0·5
Peach, whole	4oz (113g), average-sized fruit	35	1·5
Peaches, canned	4oz (113g), fruit and syrup	95	1·0
Peanuts, shelled	1oz (28g)	160	2·5
Peanut butter	½oz (14g), sufficient for one sandwich	88	1·0
Pearl barley, see Barley, pearl			
Pear, whole	5oz (142g), average-sized fruit	40	2·5
Pears, canned	4oz (113g), fruit and syrup	90	2·0
Peas			
fresh, raw	1oz (28g), salad serving	20	1·5
fresh or frozen, boiled	4oz (113g) raw weight	60	9·0
garden, canned	3½oz (99g), half the drained contents of a 10oz (283g) can	45	6·0
processed, canned	3½oz (99g)	75	7·5

dried, uncooked		
1½oz (42g), in average portion of pea soup	120	7·0
split		
2oz (56g) dry weight, amount in average portion pease pudding	175	6·5
chick		
raw	1oz (28g) dry weight	90	4·0
boiled	3oz (85g) cooked weight	90	5·0
Pepper, green		
raw	1oz (28g), salad serving	5	0·5
cooked	5oz (142g), average-sized pepper	20	1·5
Piccalilli	1oz (28g), 1 rounded tablespoon (30ml)	10	0·5
Pickle, sweet	1oz (28g), 1 rounded tablespoon (30ml)	40	0·5
Pilchards, canned in tomato sauce	2½oz (70g), average-sized pilchard	85	0
Pineapple		
fresh	2oz (56g), average slice without skin and core	25	0·5
canned in syrup	4oz (113g), fruit and syrup	90	1·0

Food	Portion	Calories	Fibre g
Plaice, fillets, fried in crumbs	6oz (170g) raw weight	435	1·0
Plums Victoria, dessert	2½oz (70g), average-sized fruit	15	1·5
cooking, stewed without sugar, weighed with stones	6oz (170g)	40	3·5
Pork chop, grilled	7oz (200g) raw weight, fat cut off after grilling	315	0
leg, roast	3oz (85g), lean only	155	0
Pork sausages, grilled	2oz (56g), large sausage, raw weight	135	0
	1oz (28g), 1 chipolata, raw weight	65	0
Porridge	1oz (28g), oatmeal or porridge oats made up with water	110	2·0
Potato baked	7oz (200g), eaten with skin	170	5·0
roast	2oz (56g)	90	1·0
instant, mashed	1oz (28g) dry weight	90	4·5

old, boiled and mashed	4oz (113g)	90	1·0
new			
boiled	4oz (113g)	85	2·5
canned	4oz (113g) drained weight	60	3·0
Prawns, shelled	2oz (56g)	60	0
Prunes, dried			
with stones	1oz (28g), four to five prunes	20	2·0
stewed without sugar	4oz (113g) cooked weight	85	8·5
Puffed wheat	¾oz (21g), average breakfast bowl	70	3·5
Rabbit, stewed	6oz (170g), weighed on the bone	150	0
Radishes, raw	1oz (28g), salad serving	5	0·5
Raisins	½oz (14g), serving with cereal etc.	35	1·0
Raspberries			
raw	4oz (113g)	30	8·5
canned in syrup	4oz (113g), fruit and syrup	95	5·5
Redcurrants, stewed without sugar	4oz (113g)	20	8·0

Food	Portion	Calories	Fibre g
Rhubarb	4oz (113g) raw weight	10	3·0
Rice Krispies	1oz (28g), average breakfast bowl	105	1·0
Rice			
brown	2oz (56g) dry weight, usual amount for a rice-based meal	200	2·5
white	2oz (56g) dry weight	205	1·5
Rock salmon, fried in batter	6oz (170g)	445	0·5
Sago	½oz (14g) raw weight, usual amount in a serving of milk pudding	50	0·5
Salad cream	1 level tablespoon (15ml)	50	0
Salad dressing, low-calorie (e.g. Waistline, Heinz)	1 level tablespoon (15ml)	25	0
Salami	1oz (28g)	135	0
Salmon, canned	3oz (85g) drained weight	170	0
Salsify, boiled	4oz (113g)	20	1·0

Food		Calories	Fibre (g)
Sardines			
canned in oil	2oz (56g), weighed after draining off oil	120	0
canned in tomato sauce	2oz (56g)	100	0
Scampi, in breadcrumbs, fried	3oz (85g)	265	1·0
Sea-kale, boiled	4oz (113g)	10	1·0
Semolina	½oz (14g) dry weight, amount in a serving of milk pudding	50	0·5
Shortcrust pastry			
white flour, cooked	1½oz (42g), usual amount in a serving of flan	220	1·0
wholemeal flour, cooked	1½oz (42g)	210	3·0
Shredded Wheat	¾oz (21g), one Shredded Wheat	70	2·5
Spaghetti			
white	2oz (56g), dry weight, usual amount in a pasta dish	210	1·5
brown wholewheat	2oz (56g) dry weight	195	5·5
canned in tomato sauce	7oz (200g), half large can	120	2·0
Spinach, boiled	4oz (113g)	30	7·0

Food	Portion	Calories	Fibre g
Spring greens, boiled	4oz (113g)	10	4·5
Spring onions	½oz (14g), salad serving	5	0·5
Strawberries, raw	4oz (113g)	30	2·5
Sugar	1 rounded teaspoon (10ml)	35	0
Sugar Puffs	1oz (28g), average breakfast bowl	95	1·5
Sultanas	½oz (14g), serving with cereal etc.	35	1·0
Sunflower seeds	¼oz (7g), just a nibble	35	0·5
Swedes, boiled	4oz (113g)	20	3·0
Sweetcorn kernels, canned	3½oz (99g)	75	5·5
Syrup, golden	1 level tablespoon (15ml)	60	0
Tangerine	3oz (85g), average-sized fruit	60	1·0
Tapioca	½oz (14g) dry weight, usual amount in a serving of milk pudding	50	0·5

Tomatoes			
fresh	4oz (113g), two, average-sized	15	1·5
canned	4oz (113g)	10	1·0
Tongue, ox, pickled, boiled	2oz (56g)	165	0
Treacle, black	1 level tablespoon (15ml)	50	0
Tripe, stewed	6oz (170g)	170	0
Trout	6oz (170g) raw weight	150	0
Tuna			
canned in brine	7oz (198g) can	230	0
canned in oil	7oz (198g) can	365	0
Turnips, boiled	4oz (113g)	15	2·5
Turkey, roast	3oz (85g), meat only, no skin	115	0
Veal			
cutlet, coated in egg and breadcrumbs, fried	3oz (85g)	180	0
fillet, roast	3oz (85g)	190	0
Vegetable oil	1 level tablespoon (15ml)	125	0

Food	Portion	Calories	Fibre g
Walnuts	1oz (28g) shelled weight	145	1·5
Watercress	1oz (28g), generous salad serving	5	1·0
Weetabix	two biscuits	115	4·5
Wheatgerm	½oz (15g), 1 rounded tablespoon (30ml)	45	0·5
Whitecurrants, stewed without sugar	4oz (113g)	25	6·5
Yogurt, low-fat			
natural	5·3oz (150g) carton	80	0
flavoured	5·3oz (150g) carton	120	0
hazelnut	5·3oz (150g) carton	160	2·5

Calorie and Fibre Guide and Chart to Packaged Foods

Calorie and Fibre Guide
to Packaged Foods

Here, available to the public for the first time, is a comprehensive guide to the useful fibre-supplying packaged foods.

Dietary fibre is not an easy substance to measure, and in order to reveal this valuable information we have had to draw on the assistance of the manufacturers themselves in some cases, and in others on the help of the technicians at London University and the analytical experts working for Dr David Southgate at the Food Research Institute.

It is important to emphasize that the values given for fibre are approximate. Fibre-measuring methods are still in their infancy. Different brands and packages of the same type of food will differ a little in their precise composition. But the figures here will provide you with a good enough guide to ensure that you reach that 30-grams-plus daily fibre total to ease and speed your slimming and help protect your health.

The quantities given in this guide are those which we feel will be most convenient to you in planning your menus. Usually we list the number of calories and the amount of dietary fibre in a whole can or package. From the weight of the can or package you will easily be able to assess whether this is an individual portion or multi-portion pack.

In the case of some foods we felt that other measures would help you more. The fibre content of different breads, for instance, is given on a per-ounce basis. Slices and sizes vary so much that it makes most sense to weigh your own average slice of your own chosen loaf to reveal the calories and fibre in that. With biscuits, the calories and dietary fibre in one or two whole biscuits is obviously of more instant value than that in a whole package. Throughout this guide we have used this kind of commonsense flexibility to make calorie- and fibre-counting easy for you.

The same principle has been applied in 'rounding off' calorie and fibre figures for easy calculation. Where the contents of a whole pack are given we round off to the nearest 5 calories and half-gram of fibre, which gives a close enough guide.

In selecting and rejecting the foods to be included in this guide we have been equally realistic. All canned fruits, for instance, will provide at least a little dietary fibre. However, with some the fibre quantity is small in relation to the calorie cost. For this reason we have listed only the canned fruits which are free of added sugar, apart from those, like raspberries and prunes, which are particularly rich sources of dietary fibre.

Canned and packaged foods can play a valuable role in modern weight-conscious and health-conscious eating – when you use the information in this guide.

Calorie and Fibre Chart of Packaged Foods

	Calories	Fibre g
Biscuits		
Bran biscuits, per biscuit		
Allinson		
Bran Biscuit	78	1·0
Bran Oatcake	39	1·0
Boots Second Nature Bran	44	1·3
Country Basket Wholewheat		
Bran	32	1·7
Crawfords Bran Oatcake	50	1·3
Fox's		
Wholemeal Bran	67	1·0
Bran Crunch	32	0·4
Holly Mill Natural Bran	33	0·8
R. M. Scott Husky Wholemeal		
Bran	37	0·2
St Michael Wholemeal Bran	65	1·0
Coconut biscuits, per biscuit		
Allinson Coconut	70	0·9
Fox's Coconut Cookies	74	0·8
Digestive biscuits, per biscuit		
Burton's Digestive Sweetmeal,		
from 200g pack	47	0·5
Hovis Digestive	56	0·7
Huntley & Palmer Digestive	63	0·5
McVitie Digestive Wheatmeal,		
from 400g pack	70	0·8
Mitchelhill's Digestive	63	0·1
Sainsbury's Sweetmeal Digestive,		
from 400g pack	60	0·5
Tesco Digestive, from 250g pack	65	0·8

	Calories	*Fibre g*
Fig biscuits, per biscuit		
Jacob's Fig Roll	**53**	**0·7**
Prewett's Fig	**60**	**0·7**
Fruit and/or nut biscuits, per biscuit		
Allinson		
Carob-coated Fruit & Nut	**62**	**0·2**
Fruit & Nut	**77**	**0·6**
Hazelnut	**63**	**0·5**
Peanut	**61**	**0·4**
Walnut	**65**	**0·5**
Boots		
Second Nature Wholemeal Fruit Bran	**33**	**1·1**
Second Nature Wholemeal Hazelnut	**37**	**0·5**
Country Basket Hazelnut	**34**	**1·2**
Fox's Oat & Fruit	**77**	**0·6**
Garibaldi biscuits, per biscuit		
Peak Frean Garibaldi	**30**	**0·3**
Muesli-type biscuits, per biscuit		
Allinson Muesli	**61**	**0·7**
Boots Second Nature Wholemeal Muesli Fruit	**38**	**0·4**
Country Basket Muesli Fruit	**37**	**1·0**
Fox's Muesli Finger	**63**	**0·7**
Oatmeal and oatflake biscuits, per biscuit		
Allinson		
Oatmeal	**74**	**0·4**
Bran Oatcake	**39**	**1·0**
Carob-coated Oatmeal	**62**	**0·2**
Country Basket Oatmeal	**34**	**1·6**
Crawford's Bran Oatcake	**50**	**1·3**

	Calories	*Fibre g*
Fox's		
Oaten Crunch	36	0·3
Oatflake Cookie	69	0·4
Oat & Fruit Biscuit	77	0·6
Paterson's		
Girdle Oatcake	50	0·5
Farmhouse Oatcake	90	0·8
Shortbread, per piece		
Allinson Wholemeal Shortbread	82	1·2
Wheaten biscuits, per biscuit		
Fox's Wheaten Cookies	69	0·5
Prewett's Wholemeal	65	0·4
Miscellaneous biscuits, per biscuit		
Allinson		
Carob-coated Ginger/Bran	61	0·4
Demerara	66	0·4
Ginger	49	0·6
Honey	57	0·7
Boots Second Nature Wholemeal		
Six Grains	37	0·4
Country Basket		
Six Grains	34	1·5
Yogurt	34	1·2
Fox's		
Fivers	85	0·8
Nice	39	0·3
Itona Granny Ann High Fibre	100	5·0
Jacob's Farmhouse	34	0·4
Mitchelhill's Healthy Life	61	0·1
Prewett's		
Carob Chip Cookies	65	0·4
Sesame & Sunflower Cookies	67	0·5
Stem Ginger Cookies	59	0·4

	Calories	Fibre g
Crispbreads and crackers, per biscuit		
Country Basket Wholewheat		
Crispbread	32	0·7
Crisp-i-Bran	19	2·9
Energen		
Brancrisp	23	1·3
Starch Reduced Bran	18	0·7
Starch Reduced Brown Wheat	17	0·4
Starch Reduced Cheese	19	0·3
Starch Reduced Rye	17	0·4
Starch Reduced Wheat	18	0·2
Jacob's		
Vitawheat	28	0·7
Vitawheat, Rye	28	0·7
Parkstone Bakeries Crackerbread	23	0·3
Primula Extra Thin	20	0·1
Ryvita		
Brown	25	0·9
Original	25	0·9
Salt-free	25	0·9

Brans

Soya brans, per oz (28g)		
Direct Foods Soya Bran	24	9·9
Granose Soya Bran	60	9·9

Wheat brans, per oz (28g)		
Allinson		
Bran Plus	63	7·1
Broad Bran	43	12·5
Boots Second Nature Natural		
Unprocessed Bran	56	12·4
Itona Wheat Bran	43	12·5
Prewett's Natural Wheat Bran	43	12·5

	Calories	*Fibre g*
Breads		

Bran loaves, per oz (28g)		
Nimble Family Bran	**70**	**1.3**
Sunblest Hi Bran	**57**	**3·1**
Sunblest Sunbran	**62**	**1·3**
Windmill Bran	**64**	**1·8**

Granary, per oz (28g)		
Windmill Granary	**67**	**1·6**

Wheatgerm loaves, per oz (28g)		
Hovis		
Family Loaf	**63**	**1·4**
Handy Loaf	**66**	**1·4**
Original	**66**	**1·4**
Vitbe Wheatgerm	**65**	**1·4**

Wheatmeal (brown) loaves, per oz (28g)		
Mothers Pride Brown Long Loaf	**64**	**1·6**
Windmill Country Brown	**64**	**1·6**

White loaves, per oz (28g)		
Mothers Pride		
Danish Toaster	**71**	**0·9**
Danish White	**71**	**0·9**
White Long Loaf	**66**	**0·8**
Nimble		
Family White	**71**	**0·9**
Long White	**74**	**0·8**
Sunblest White	**65**	**0·8**
Windmill White Fibre	**64**	**1·7**

Wholemeal loaves, per oz (28g)		
Allinson Wholemeal	**61**	**2·4**
Windmill		
Wholemeal, small loaf, 400g	**64**	**2·6**
Wholemeal, large loaf, 800g	**61**	**2·4**

	Calories	Fibre g
Bread rolls, per oz (28g)		
Granose Wheatmeal Rolls	100	1·0
Granose White Rolls	101	0·5
Bread mixes, per packet dry mix		
Allinson		
Bran Bread Mix, 1¼lb pack	2,050	75·0
Wholewheat Bread Mix, 1¼lb pack	1,845	57·0
Prewett's Ever-ready Bread Mix,		
1¼lb pack	1,895	48·0

Breakfast Cereals

	Calories	Fibre g
Maize (corn) breakfast cereals, per oz (28g)		
Cornflakes, *see* Your Basic Calorie and Fibre Chart		
Kellogg's		
Crunchy Nut Corn Flakes	107	0·5
Frosties	100	0·3
Muesli-type and crunchy breakfast cereals, per oz (28g)		
except where stated		
Boots		
Second Nature Honey Muesli	118	2·2
Second Nature Muesli	103	2·1
Cheshire		
Wholefoods Muesli	104	0·8
Wholefoods Economy Muesli	93	0·5
Familia		
Birchermuesli	115	2·0
Muesli (Swiss Mixed Cereal),		
1 portion pack, 2½oz (71g)	285	5·5
Holly Mill		
Muesli	103	1·8
Muesli Base	101	2·1
Sugar Free Muesli	98	2·0
Jordans		
Country Muesli	103	0·7
Muesli Tub, Banana and Brazil,		
2½oz (71g) tub	305	3·6

	Calories	*Fibre g*
Muesli Tub, Coconut and Sultana, 2½oz (71g) tub	260	3·6
Muesli Tub, Date and Cashew, 2½oz (71g) tub	263	3·6
Original Crunchy Natural	123	0·4
Original Crunchy with Honey, Almonds and Raisins	121	0·4
Original Crunchy with Bran and Apple	116	0·7
Kellogg's Country Store	100	1·4
Prewett's		
Bran Muesli	87	6·2
Honey Muesli	104	1·8
Muesli Base	105	2·1
Muesli Deluxe	111	2·1
Muesli	102	1·9
Quaker		
Harvest Crunch	126	2·8
Harvest Crunch, Bran & Apple	129	4·3
Safeway Swiss Style Breakfast Cereal	110	2·0
Sainsbury's Swiss Style Breakfast Cereal	100	2·0
Sunwheel Natural Foods Fruit and Nut Muesli	103	3·0
Tesco Swiss Style Breakfast Cereal	105	2·0
Weetabix Alpen	105	1·9
Oat breakfast cereals, per oz (28g)		
Boots Second Nature Bran & Oat Crunch	103	5·4
Lyons Tetley		
Ready Brek, Butter Flavour	110	2·2
Ready Brek, Standard Flavour	110	2·2
Prewett's		
Breakfast Oats	115	2·0
Oatmeal, fine/medium/coarse	115	2·0
Porridge, wheatmeal	95	2·7

	Calories	Fibre g
Oat breakfast cereals, *cont.*		
Quaker		
Golden Oaties	107	2·3
Oats	105	4·3
Oat Krunchies	108	3·4
Warm Start	107	4·3
Safeway		
Hot Oat Cereal	115	2·2
Quick Cooking Oats	105	4·0
Sainsbury's Scotch Porridge		
Oats	105	4·0
Scotts Porage Oats	115	4·0
Tesco		
Instant Oats	115	2·2
Scotch Porridge Oats	115	4·0
Waitrose Instant Porridge	115	2·2
Whitworth's Porridge Oats	114	2·0
Rice breakfast cereals, per oz (28g)		
Kellogg's		
Rice Krispies	99	0·3
Ricicles	100	0·3
Coco Pops	101	0·3
Puffa Puffa Rice	117	0·1
Wheat (including bran) breakfast cereals, per oz (28g) except where stated		
Allinson Crunchy Bran	64	7·7
Boots Second Nature Bran & Oat		
Crunch	103	5·4
Energen		
Brancrunch	115	4·3
Wheatflakes	100	4·2
Granose		
Fruit Bran	86	3·5
Sunnybisk, each	50	1·1
Holly Mill Wheat-Heart	117	1·0

	Calories	*Fibre g*
Kellogg's		
All-Bran	**70**	**8·0**
Bran Buds	**74**	**7·4**
Bran Flakes	**85**	**4·2**
Sultana Bran	**82**	**3·6**
Smacks	**106**	**2·0**
Meadow Farm Toasted Bran	**100**	**8·2**
Nabisco		
Bran Flakes	**105**	**3·4**
Shredded Wheat, each	**80**	**2·4**
Shreddies	**105**	**2·3**
Spoonsize	**100**	**3·1**
Prewett's Whole Wheat Flakes	**102**	**2·6**
Quaker		
Puffed Wheat	**106**	**4·3**
Sugar Puffs	**104**	**2·1**
Safeway Biskwheat, each	**68**	**2·5**
Sainsbury's		
Puffed Wheat	**100**	**4·3**
Whole Wheat Bisk, each	**70**	**2·5**
Weetabix		
Bran Fare	**75**	**8·2**
Farmhouse Bran	**85**	**5·7**
Weetabix, per biscuit	**58**	**2·2**
Weetaflakes	**96**	**3·6**
Miscellaneous breakfast cereals, per oz (28g)		
Bird's Grape-Nuts	**99**	**2·0**
Holly Mill		
Day Brek	**118**	**5·2**
Bran Brek	**123**	**2·3**
Kellogg's Special K	**101**	**0·5**
Prewett's Golden Grains	**105**	**1·6**
Pronutro	**105**	**3·4**

Chutneys and Pickles

Bicks Corn Relish, per oz (28g)	**30**	**1·3**

	Calories	Fibre g
Chutneys and Pickles, *cont.*		
Happy Farm		
Piccalilli, per oz (28g)	9	0·5
Sweet Pickle, per oz (28g)	38	0·5
Tomato & Apple Chutney, per oz (28g)	48	0·5

Dehydrated Meals

	Calories	Fibre g
Vesta Chilli con Carne with Rice,		
pack, serves two	800	19·0

Flour

	Calories	Fibre g
Rye flour, per oz (28g)		
Prewett's Rye Flour	96	0·3
Soya flour, per oz (28g)		
Prewett's Soya Flour	123	3·4
White flour (plain, self-raising and strong flours), per oz (28g)		
Allinson		
81% Farmhouse (plain)	100	2·3
81% Farmhouse (self-raising)	100	2·3
Strong White	97	1·1
Prewett's		
Millstone Flour 81% (plain)	97	2·3
Millstone Flour 81% (self-raising)	100	2·3
Strong White Bread Flour		
(unbleached)	97	1·1
Super White Unbleached Flour		
(plain)	97	1·4
Super White Unbleached Flour		
(self-raising)	97	1·1
Whitworths		
Plain White Flour	99	1·0
Self-Raising White Flour	96	1·0
Wholemeal flour		
Allinson		
100% Wholemeal Flour (plain)	96	3·1

	Calories	*Fibre g*
Cerea 100% Flour	96	3·1
Boots Second Nature Stoneground Wholemeal Flour	89	2·7
Jordans 100% Wholewheat Flour	91	0·7
Prewett's		
100% Organic Wholemeal Flour	96	3·1
100% Wholemeal Flour (plain)	96	3·1
100% Wholemeal Flour (self-raising)	96	3·1

Fruit, Canned

Apples
Waitrose Apple Slices in Natural Juice, 7¾oz (219g) can	75	4·5

Apricots
Boots Shapers Apricots in Low-calorie Syrup, 7¾oz (220g) can	35	3·0
Dietade Apricots in Water, 7oz (198g) can	35	2·5
Frank Cooper's Apricots in Water, 7oz (198g) can	25	2·5
Sainsbury's Apricot Halves in Apple Juice, 14½oz (411g) can	185	5·5

Blackberries
Sainsbury's Blackberries in Syrup, 7½oz (213g) can	210	10·5
Smedley Blackberries in Syrup, 7½oz (213g) can	145	10·0
Weight Watchers Blackberries in Low-calorie Syrup, 7oz (198g) can	50	10·0

Blackcurrants
Ribena Blackcurrants in Syrup, 300g can	345	13·0
Sainsbury's Blackcurrants in Syrup, 7½oz (213g) can	210	9·0
Smedley Blackcurrants in Syrup, 7½oz (213g) can	145	9·0

	Calories	Fibre g
Fruit salad		
Dietade		
Fruit Salad in Water, 7oz (198g) can	35	2·0
Fruit Salad in Fruit-sugar Syrup,		
8oz (227g) can	90	2·5
Frank Cooper's Fruit Salad in Water,		
7oz (198g) can	35	2·0
Weight Watchers Fruit Salad in		
Low-calorie Syrup, 7oz (198g) can	35	2·0
Gooseberries		
Hartley's Gooseberries,		
10oz (283g) can	240	5·5
Safeway Gooseberries, 10oz (283g) can	180	5·5
Sainsbury's Gooseberries,		
10½oz (298g) can	210	6·0
Smedley Gooseberries, 10oz (283g) can	180	5·0
Grapefruit		
John West Grapefruit Segments in		
Natural Juice, 10oz (283g) can	120	1·0
Libby's Grapefruit Segments,		
sweetened, 19oz (538g) can	380	2·0
Princes Grapefruit Segments,		
10oz (283g) can	170	1·0
Sainsbury's Grapefruit Segments in		
Natural Juice, 19oz (539g) can	210	2·0
Tesco Grapefruit Segments,		
sweetened, 19oz (539g) can	340	2·0
Waitrose Grapefruit in Natural Juice,		
7¾oz (219g) can	75	1·0
Weight Watchers Grapefruit		
Segments in Low-calorie Syrup		
7oz (198g) can	50	1·0
Loganberries		
Tesco Loganberries in Syrup,		
14½oz (411g)	320	13·5

	Calories	Fibre g
Mandarin oranges		
John West Mandarin Orange Segments in Natural Juice, 10½oz (298g) can	80	1·0
Peaches		
Boots Shapers Peachers in Low-calorie Syrup, 7¾oz (220g) can	45	2·0
Dietade Peaches in Water, 7oz (198g) can	35	2·0
Frank Cooper's Peaches in Water, 7oz (198g) can	35	2·0
John West Peach Slices in Fruit Juice, 10oz (283g) can	130	3·0
Koo Peach Slices in Apple Juice, 8oz (227g) can	95	2·5
Sainsbury's Peaches in Apple Juice, 14½oz (411g) can	185	4·0
Waitrose Peaches in Apple Juice, 7¾oz (219g) can	75	2·0
Weight Watchers Peaches in Low-calorie Syrup, 7oz (198g) can	40	2·0
Pears		
Boots Shapers Pears in Low-calorie Syrup, 7¾oz (220g) can	50	3·5
Dietade		
Pears in Water, 7oz (198g) can	35	3·5
Pears in Fruit-sugar Syrup, 8oz (227g) can	95	4·0
Frank Cooper's Pears in Water, 7oz (198g) can	35	3·5
John West Pear Quarters in Fruit Juice, 10oz (283g) can	110	5·0
Koo Pear Halves in Apple Juice, 8oz (227g) can	105	4·0
Sainsbury's Pear Halves in Apple Juice, 14½oz (411g) can	185	7·0

	Calories	*Fibre g*
Pears, *cont.*		
Waitrose Pears in Apple Juice, 7¾oz (219g) can	75	3·5
Weight Watchers Pears in Low-calorie Syrup, 7oz (198g) can	40	3·5
Pineapple		
Boots Shapers Pineapple in Low-calorie Syrup, 7¾oz (220g) can	55	2·0
Del Monte Pineapple Slices in Natural Juice, 8oz (227g) can	150	2·0
Dietade		
Pineapple in Water, 7oz (198g) can	35	2·0
Pineapple in Fruit-sugar Syrup, 8oz (227g) can	100	2·0
Frank Cooper's Pineapple in Water, 7oz (198g) can	40	2·0
John West Pineapple Rings in Natural Juice, 8oz (227g) can	130	2·0
Sainsbury's Pineapple Slices in Natural Juice, 8oz (227g) can	105	2·0
Waitrose Pineapple in Natural Juice, 8oz (227g) can	120	2·0
Weight Watchers Pineapple Rings in Low-calorie Syrup, 7oz (198g) can	70	2·0
Prunes		
Pickering Prunes in Syrup, 7½oz (213g) can	220	7·5
Tesco Prunes in Syrup, 7½oz (213g) can	235	9·0
Raspberries		
Baxters		
Raspberries in Syrup, 10¼oz (290g) can	250	14·5
Raspberries in Syrup, 15oz (425g) can	365	21·0

	Calories	*Fibre g*
Hartleys Raspberries in Syrup, 15oz (425g) can	**400**	**21·0**
Sainsbury's Raspberries in Syrup, 7½oz (213g) can	**155**	**10·5**
Smedley Raspberries in Syrup, 7½oz (213g) can	**155**	**9·0**
Weight Watchers Raspberries in Low-calorie Syrup, 7oz (198g) can	**50**	**10·0**

Strawberries
Baxters

	Calories	*Fibre g*
Strawberries in Syrup, 10¼oz (290g) can	**250**	**3·0**
Strawberries in Syrup, 15oz (425g) can	**365**	**4·0**
Weight Watchers Strawberries in Low-calorie Syrup, 7oz (198g) can	**50**	**2·0**

Fruit, Dried

Whitworths

	Calories	*Fibre g*
Apricots, no-need-to-soak, 8·8oz (250g)	**385**	**52·5**
Chopped Dates, sugar rolled, 8·8oz (250g)	**680**	**17·5**
Dessert Dates, with stones, 8·8oz (250g)	**530**	**18·5**
Stoned Dates, 8·8oz (250g)	**620**	**21·5**
Figs, 8·8oz (250g)	**450**	**37·5**
Prunes, no-need-to-soak, 8·8oz (250g)	**290**	**30·0**

Pasta

Wholewheat Pasta, per oz (28g)

	Calories	*Fibre g*
Newform Foods Limited Country Basket Spaghetti	**99**	**2·3**
Record Whole Wheat Lasagne, uncooked	**105**	**2·8**

	Calories	Fibre g
Wholewheat Pasta (Record), *cont*.		
Whole Wheat Long Spaghetti, uncooked	105	2·8
Whole Wheat Short Cut Macaroni, uncooked	105	2·8
Whole Wheat Spaghetti Rings, uncooked	105	2·8

Rice

Brown Rice, per oz (28g)		
Prewett's Unpolished Rice, long/short grain	97	1·4
Whitworths Brown Rice	102	0·3

White Rice, per oz (28g)		
Kellogg's Boil-in-bag rice, uncooked	93	0·1
Whitworths		
Basmati Rice, uncooked	103	0·1
Ground Rice, uncooked	103	0·1
Rice, long/short grain, uncooked	103	0·1
Rice Easy Cook, uncooked	105	0·1

Savoury Pot Snacks

Noodle snacks, per pot made up		
Golden Wonder		
Beef & Tomato Pot Noodle	370	1·5
Cheese & Tomato Pot Noodle	345	2·0
Chicken & Mushroom Pot Noodle	380	8·5
Spicy Curry Pot Noodle	380	4·5
Sweet & Sour Pot Noodle	345	1·0

Rice snacks, per pot made up		
Golden Wonder		
Chicken Curry	265	2·5
Chicken Risotto	270	1·0

	Calories	*Fibre g*
Savoury Beef	**255**	**1·5**
Spicy Tomato	**250**	**1·5**

Slimmers Products

Meal replacements
Balance, per serving

(26g) with 175ml milk	**198**	**2·0**
Crunch'n'Slim		
Coconut & Currant Bars, per meal	**230**	**2·8**
Orange & Raisin Bars, per meal	**230**	**2·8**
Sultana & Hazelnut Bars, per meal	**230**	**2·8**
Limits		
Cheese Flavour Cracker Biscuits with Bran	**250**	**2·5**
Chocolate Biscuits with Bran	**250**	**2·5**
Chocolate Flavour Wafer with Bran	**250**	**2·5**
Chocolate Mint Biscuits with Bran	**250**	**2·5**
Coffee Flavour Biscuits with Bran	**250**	**2·5**
Lemon & Lime Flavour Biscuits with Bran	**250**	**2·5**
Milk Chocolate Sweetmeal Biscuits with Bran	**250**	**2·5**
Orange Flavour Biscuits with bran	**250**	**2·5**
Plain Sweetmeal Digestive with Bran	**250**	**2·5**
Vanilla Flavour Biscuits with Bran	**250**	**2·5**
SlimGard, per daily quota of 1 Bar, 1 Drink and 2 Inbetweeners	**333**	**1·7**

Starch-reduced rolls

Energen Starch Reduced Rolls, each	**23**	**0·5**

Snacks

Cereal, fruit & nut bars and slices, per bar or slice
Holly Mill

Carob Chip Bar	**145**	**0·5**

	Calories	*Fibre g*
Cereal, fruit & nut bars and slices (Holly Mill), *cont.*		
Cereal & Nut Crunchy Bar	115	0·5
Crunchy Slice	185	1·0
Fruit & Nut Slice	175	1·0
Muesli Slice	215	1·0
Oat, Apple & Raisin Slice	165	1·0
Oat, Apricot & Almond Slice	175	1·0
Protein Slice	175	0·5
Roasted Peanut Bar	155	0·5
Sesame Bar	125	1·0
Jordans		
Original Crunchy Bar, Honey & Almond	150	0·5
Original Crunchy Bar, Honey & Coconut	145	1·0
Lynn Valley Wholefoods, Peanut & Raisin Bar	170	2·5
Prewett's		
Apple & Date Dessert Bar	120	4·0
Banana Dessert Bar	75	2·5
Date & Fig Dessert Bar	125	3·5
Fruit & Bran Bar	85	5·0
Fruit & Nut Dessert Bar	130	4·0
Muesli Fruit Bar	125	3·5
Quaker		
Harvest Crunch Bar, Almond Variety	90	1·0
Harvest Crunch Bar, Peanut Variety	90	1·0
Fruit and nut mixtures		
Cheshire Wholefoods		
Trail Pack, Fruit & Nut Mix, 100g pack	535	5·0
Trail Pack with coconut and banana, 56g pack	240	3·0
T. G. Smith (Liverpool) Limited		
Tropical Treat, 100g pack	410	8·0

	Calories	*Fibre g*
Savoury snacks		
Allinson Wheateats, per 21g packet	90	0·5
Soups		
Lentil		
Baxter's Lentil, 15oz (425g) can	200	9·0
Campbell's		
Condensed Lentil, 4·9oz (140g) can,		
makes 9·8oz (280g)	130	5·5
Condensed Lentil, 10½oz (298g) can,		
makes 21oz (596g)	280	12·0
Granny Soup, Lentil,		
15oz (425g) can	240	10·0
Heinz Lentil, 10·6oz (300g) can	180	6·0
Minestrone		
Batchelor's Minestrone, packet,		
makes 1 pint	155	2·5
Crosse & Blackwell Box Soup,		
Minestrone, makes 1 pint	80	3·5
Knorr Minestrone, packet,		
makes 1½ pints	225	4·5
Sainsbury's Minestrone, packet,		
makes 1 pint	120	4·0
Pea		
Baxter's Pea & Ham, 15oz (425g)	225	10·0
Campbell's		
Condensed Pea & Ham,		
10½oz (298g) can, makes 21oz (596g)	400	13·0
Main Course Pea & Ham,		
15oz (425g) can	350	9·0
Heinz Pea & Ham, 10·6oz (300g) can	200	7·0
Vegetable		
Heinz Vegetable & Lentil Big Soup,		
15·3oz (435g) can	210	8·9

	Calories	Fibre g
Soya and Cereal Protein Foods		

Savoury mixes, per packet or can unless stated otherwise

Brooke Bond Oxo

	Calories	Fibre g
Beanfeast, Bolognese, 4oz (113g) pack	330	10·0
Beanfeast, Mexican Chilli, 4oz (113g) pack	330	17·0
Beanfeast, Mild Curry, 4oz (113g) pack	320	10·0
Beanfeast, Paella Style, 4oz (113g) pack	350	13·5
Beanfeast, Soya Mince with Onion, 4oz (113g) pack	375	10·0
Beanfeast, Supreme, 4oz (113g) pack	335	13·5

Direct Foods

	Calories	Fibre g
Protoveg, Natural, Unflavoured, 4½oz (127g) carton	370	4·0
Protoveg, Flavoured (Beef, Ham, Pork Style), 4½oz (127g) carton	360	4·5
Protoveg Menu, Farmhouse Soya Stew Mince, 4oz (113g) carton	405	3·5
Protoveg Menu, Minced Soya & Onion Mix, 5oz (142g) carton	510	3·5
Protoveg Menu, Soya Bolognese Mix, 4oz (113g) carton	390	5·5
Protoveg Menu, Soya Mince with Vegetables, 4oz (113g) carton	395	4·0
Protoveg Menu, Burgamix, 6½oz (184g) pack	995	9·0
Protoveg Menu, Sosmix, 6½oz (184g) pack	960	5·5
Protoveg Menu, Jumbo Grills, 8oz (227g) carton	750	4·0
Protoveg Menu, Jumbo Grills Flavouring, per oz (28g)	68	0·7

	Calories	*Fibre g*
Protoveg Menu, Vegetable Curry, 112g pack	**400**	**4·0**
Protoveg Menu, Vegetable Goulash, 112g pack	**395**	**3·5**
Mr Fritzi Fry's Sausage Mix, 8oz (227g) pack	**1,210**	**13·0**
Mr Fritzi Fry's Savoury Mix (Burga Style), 8oz (227g) pack	**1,075**	**8·0**
Mr Fritzi Fry's Hawaiian Croquettes (Fishcake Style), 8oz (227g) pack	**850**	**7·5**
Granose		
Beef Flavour Chunks, per oz (28g) dry weight	**95**	**0·9**
Beef Flavour Mince, per oz (28g) dry weight	**95**	**0·9**
Bologna, 10oz (283g) can	**475**	**4·0**
Bologna, 15oz (425g) can	**710**	**6·5**
Bolognese Sauce, 10oz (284g) can	**170**	**1·5**
Cannelloni, 14oz (397g) can	**300**	**1·0**
Chicken Flavour Pie Filling, 10oz (284g) can	**165**	**1·5**
Goulash, 10oz (284g) can	**155**	**1·5**
Nutloaf, 15oz (425g) can	**750**	**14·5**
Nuttolene, 15oz (425g) can	**1,265**	**14·5**
Protose, 15oz (425g) can	**675**	**14·5**
Ravioli, 15oz (425g) can	**270**	**2·5**
Sausalatas, 10oz (284g) can	**390**	**4·0**
Sausalatas, 15oz (425g) can	**580**	**6·0**
Sausalene, 10oz (284g) can	**555**	**7·5**
Sausfry, per oz (28g) dry weight	**140**	**2·6**
Saviand, 10oz (284g) can	**565**	**4·5**
Savoury Cuts, 7½oz (213g) can	**185**	**0·5**
Savoury Cuts, 15oz (425g) can	**375**	**1·0**
Savoury Pudding, 11oz (312g) can	**645**	**4·5**
Savoury Pudding, Chicken Flavour, 11oz (312g) can	**510**	**3·0**

	Calories	Fibre g
Savoury mixes (Granose), *cont.*		
Soya Beans in Tomato Sauce, 7½oz (213g) can	365	7·5
Soya Beans in Tomato Sauce, 15oz (425g) can	725	15·5
Tenderbits, 7½oz (213g) can	170	0·5
Vegetable Pâté, per oz (28g)	85	1·0
Prewett's		
5 Cereal Savoury Mix, per oz (28g) dry weight	97	2·5
5 Cereal Savoury Mix, 300g pack	1,025	24·0

Spreads

	Calories	Fibre g
Sunwheel Natural Foods		
Peanut Butter, Crunchy and Smooth, per oz (28g)	169	1·4
Sesame Spread, per oz (28g)	177	1·6
Sunflower Spread, per oz (28g)	175	1·1

Vegetables, Canned

	Calories	Fibre g
Artichoke hearts		
Wardour Artichoke Hearts, 14oz (400g)	115	2·5
Baked beans with tomato sauce		
Armour Baked Beans with Tomato Sauce, 7¾oz (220g)	140	16·0
Chef Baked Beans with 4 Pork Sausages, 7¾oz (220g)	270	13·5
Crosse & Blackwell Baked Beans with Tomato Sauce, 15½oz (439g)	280	32·0
Heinz		
Baked Beans with Tomato Sauce, 5·29oz (150g)	110	11·0

	Calories	Fibre g
Baked Beans with Tomato Sauce, 7·9oz (225g)	160	16·5
Baked Beans with Tomato Sauce, 15·9oz (450g)	325	33·5
Baked Beans with Pork Sausages, 7·9oz (225g)	285	11·5
Curried Beans with Sultanas, 7·9oz (225g)	195	16·5
S & W Barbecue Beans Chuckwagon Style in Tomato Sauce, 15½oz (439g)	315	33·0
Safeway		
Baked Beans with Tomato Sauce, 7¾oz (220g)	140	16·0
Baked Beans with Tomato Sauce, 15¾oz (447g)	285	32·5
Sainsbury's		
Baked Beans with Tomato Sauce, 7¾oz (220g)	155	16·0
Baked Beans and Sausages, 7¾oz (220g)	340	12·0
Tesco Baked Beans, 15oz (425g)	270	31·0
Waitrose Baked Beans, 5½oz (156g)	100	11·5
Barlotti beans		
Vulcano Barlotti Beans, 15oz (425g)	215	17·0
Broad beans		
Hartley's Broad Beans, 10oz (283g)	100	7·5
Smedley Broad Beans, 10oz (283g)	90	7·5
Waitrose Broad Beans, 10oz (283g)	120	10·5
Butter beans		
Batchelor's Butter Beans, 7½oz (213g)	115	6·5
Hartley's Butter Beans, 10oz (283g)	175	8·5
Safeway Butter Beans, 7½oz (213g)	115	6·5
Sainsbury's Butter Beans, 7¾oz (220g)	125	6·5
Tesco Butter Beans, 7½oz (213g)	125	7·0

	Calories	*Fibre g*
Cannellini beans (white kidney beans)		
Batchelor's Cannellini Beans, 7·9oz (223g)	**125**	**10·0**
Bonduelle White Kidney Beans in Tomato Sauce, 14½oz (411g)	**295**	**20·0**
Vulcano White Kidney (Cannellini), 15oz (425g)	**240**	**18·5**
Green beans		
Bonduelle		
Golden, Cut, 7¼oz (205g)	**25**	**4·5**
Whole Green Beans, 14½oz (411g)	**20**	**9·5**
Heley Cut Green Beans, 14½oz (411g)	**50**	**7·5**
Safeway		
Sliced Green Beans, 9½oz (269g)	**20**	**3·5**
Whole Green Beans, 14oz (397g)	**15**	**7·0**
Sainsbury's		
Cut Green Beans, 10oz (283g)	**30**	**5·5**
Cut Stringless Green Beans, 14oz (397g)	**40**	**7·5**
Smedley Cut Green Beans, 10oz (283g)	**15**	**5·0**
Talpe Cut Green Beans, 14oz (397g)	**35**	**6·5**
Tesco Cut Green Beans, 10oz (283g)	**30**	**5·5**
Lima beans		
S & W Lima Beans, 16oz (454g)	**310**	**26·5**
Red kidney beans		
Batchelor's Red Kidney Beans, 7·9oz (223g)	**120**	**9·5**
Pickerings Red Kidney Beans, 15·9oz (450g)	**240**	**19·0**
S & W Red Kidney Beans, 8¾oz (248g)	**130**	**11·5**
Sainsbury's Red Kidney Beans, 15½oz (439g)	**230**	**19·0**
Smedley Red Kidney Beans, 10oz (283g)	**260**	**20·0**

	Calories	*Fibre g*
Stokeley Red Kidney Beans, 15oz (425g)	**225**	**18·0**
Tesco Red Kidney Beans, 15oz (425g)	**285**	**19·5**
Beetroot Baxter's		
Baby Beets, pickled, 12oz (340g)	**155**	**8·5**
Sliced Beets, pickled, 11¾oz (333g)	**100**	**5·7**
Brussels sprouts Bonduelle Brussels Sprouts, 14½oz (411g)	**50**	**8·5**
Talpe Continental Cuisine Brussels Sprouts, 14oz (397g)	**45**	**7·5**
Carrots Sainsbury's		
Sliced Carrots, 10½oz (298g)	**35**	**6·5**
Whole Carrots, 10½oz (298g)	**30**	**6·5**
Young Carrots, 7oz (198g)	**25**	**4·5**
Smedley		
Sliced Carrots, 10½oz (298g)	**35**	**6·5**
Whole Carrots, 10½oz (298g)	**30**	**6·5**
Mixed vegetables Sainsbury's Mixed Vegetables (peas, carrots, turnips, potato), 10½oz (298g)	**95**	**9·5**
Smedley Mixed Vegetables (peas, swede, potato, carrot), 10oz (283g)	**125**	**7·0**
Tesco Mixed Vegetables (peas, carrots, potato, swede), 10oz (283g)	**125**	**7·0**
Mushrooms Chesswood		
Button Mushrooms in Brine, 7½oz (213g)	**15**	**3·0**

	Calories	*Fibre g*
Mushrooms (Chesswood), *cont*.		
Sliced Large Mushrooms in Brine, 7½oz (213g)	15	4·0
Sliced Mushrooms in Creamed Sauce, 7½oz (213g)	190	2·0
Small Whole Mushrooms in Brine, 7½oz (213g)	15	3·0
Sainsbury's Small Whole Mushrooms, 7½oz (213g)	15	3·5
Talpe Continental Cuisine Mushrooms, 7oz (198g)	15	3·0
Chick peas		
Bonduelle Chick Peas, 400g	275	14·5
Napolina Chick Peas, 15oz (425g)	275	14·5
Vulcano Chick Peas, 15oz (425g)	270	14·5
Garden peas and petit pois		
Bonduelle Petit Pois, 14½oz (411g)	125	13·5
Hartley's Garden Peas, 10oz (283g)	85	11·5
Safeway Petit Pois, 7oz (198g)	55	8·5
Sainsbury's		
Garden Peas, 5oz (142g)	45	6·5
Garden Peas, 10oz (283g)	90	13·0
Smedley		
Garden Peas, 5oz (142g)	60	4·5
Garden Peas, 10oz (283g)	125	9·5
Tesco		
Garden Peas, 10oz (283g)	85	13·0
Petit Pois, 10oz (283g)	90	13·0
Mushy peas		
Batchelor's Mushy Peas, 10·7oz (304g)	240	22·0
Sainsbury's Mushy Processed Peas, 10oz (283g)	220	23·0
Smedley Mushy Processed Peas, 10oz (283g)	240	9·0

	Calories	*Fibre g*
Tesco Mushy Processed Peas, 10oz (283g)	**225**	**23·5**
Pease pudding Pickering's		
Pease Pudding, 7½oz (213g)	**290**	**11·0**
Pease Pudding, 15oz (425g)	**585**	**21·5**
Sainsbury's		
Pease Pudding, 7¾oz (220g)	**290**	**11·0**
Pease Pudding, 15½oz (439g)	**605**	**22·5**
Processed and marrowfat peas Batchelor's Bigga Processed Peas, 10oz (283g)	**150**	**15·0**
Farrow's Giant Marrowfat Processed Peas, 4·97oz (141g)	**70**	**6·5**
International Processed Peas, 10oz (283g)	**115**	**13·5**
Safeway		
Marrowfat Processed Peas, 10oz (283g)	**115**	**13·0**
Processed Peas, 10oz (283g)	**130**	**14·0**
Sainsbury's		
Processed Peas, 10oz (283g)	**130**	**14·0**
Small Processed Peas, 10oz (283g)	**145**	**14·5**
Smedley Processed Peas, 10oz (283g)	**190**	**10·5**
Tesco Processed Peas, 10oz (283g)	**140**	**15·5**
Potatoes Sainsbury's New Potatoes, 10oz (283g)	**115**	**5·5**
Smedley New Potatoes, 10oz (283g)	**135**	**3·5**
Yeoman New Potatoes, mint flavour, 539g	**190**	**9·0**
Spinach Bonduelle		
Chopped Spinach, 7¼oz (205g)	**55**	**11·5**
Leaf Spinach, 14½oz (411g)	**65**	**13·5**

	Calories	*Fibre g*
Spinach, *cont.*		
Lockwood's Leaf Spinach, 9½oz (269g)	**40**	**7·0**
Smedley Spinach, chopped leaf,		
9oz (258g)	**30**	**7·5**
Talpe Chopped Spinach, 14oz (397g)	**90**	**20·0**
Sweetcorn		
Bonduelle Sweetcorn Kernels,		
12oz (340g)	**220**	**16·5**
Green Giant		
Mexicorn Golden Corn,		
whole kernels with peppers,		
7oz (198g)	**150**	**10·5**
Niblets Golden Corn, whole kernel,		
7oz (198g)	**150**	**11·0**
Kounty Kist Sweetcorn Kernels,		
12oz (340g)	**200**	**17·5**
Mexicana Sweetcorn with Peppers,		
11½oz (325g)	**200**	**15·0**
Sainsbury's		
Sweetcorn & Peppers, 12oz (340g)	**230**	**17·5**
Whole Kernel Sweetcorn, 7oz (198g)	**150**	**11·5**
Whole Kernel Sweetcorn,		
11½oz (326g)	**250**	**18·5**
Tesco Sweetcorn Kernels, 12oz (340g)	**260**	**18·0**
Tomatoes		
Mon Jardin Chopped Tomatoes,		
14oz (400g)	**50**	**3·5**
Napolina		
Peeled Plum Tomatoes, 8oz (227g)	**25**	**2·0**
Peeled Plum Tomatoes, 14oz (397g)	**50**	**3·5**
Regatta		
Italian Peeled Tomatoes, 8oz (227g)	**25**	**2·0**
Italian Peeled Tomatoes, 14oz (397g)	**50**	**3·5**
Sainsbury's Israeli Peeled Tomatoes,		
1lb 3oz (539g)	**65**	**5·0**

	Calories	*Fibre g*
Salads		
Bonduelle Mexican Salad		
(sweetcorn, peas, peppers),		
14½oz (411g)	165	15·5
Green Giant American Bean Salad,		
1lb 1oz (482g)	245	13·5
Heinz Vegetable Salad, 7¼oz (206g)	305	5·0

Vegetables, Dried

	Calories	*Fibre g*
Whitworths		
Mixed Vegetables, per oz (28g) dry	75	7·0
Mushrooms, per oz (28g) dry	40	7·5
Peppers, per oz (28g) dry	60	3·5
Sliced Onion, per oz (28g) dry	85	4·5

Vegetables, Frozen

For basic frozen vegetables (e.g. peas) refer to Your Basic Calorie and Fibre Chart.

	Calories	*Fibre g*
Stir-fry vegetables		
Birds Eye		
Continental Stir Fry Vegetables,		
10oz (284g), after frying	250	6·5
Country Style Stir Fry Vegetables,		
10oz (284g), after frying	250	6·5
Mediterranean Stir Fry Vegetables,		
10oz (284g), after frying	300	6·5
St Michael		
Brown Pack, 10oz (284g), as sold	90	6·0
Red Pack, 10oz (284g), as sold	80	10·0
Yellow Pack, 10oz (284g), as sold	130	8·0
Vegetable mixtures		
Birds Eye		
Casserole Vegetables, 8oz (227g)	80	5·5
Cauliflower, Peas and Carrots,		
8oz (227g)	80	9·5

	Calories	Fibre g
Vegetable mixtures (Birds Eye), *cont.*		
Original Mixed Vegetables, 4oz (113g)	60	5·5
Original Mixed Vegetables, 8oz (227g)	120	11·0
Peas, Sweetcorn and Peppers, 8oz (227g)	120	13·0
Rice, Peas and Mushrooms, 8oz (227g)	350	9·5
Rice, Sweetcorn and Peppers, 8oz (227g)	340	5·0
Ross		
Farmhouse Mixed Vegetables, 8oz (227g)	115	11·0
Mixed Vegetables, 8oz (227g)	125	12·5
Stewpack, 8oz (227g)	40	4·5
Wheatgerm		
Wheatgerm, per oz (28g)		
Allinson Wheatgerm (stabilized)	89	0·7
Bemax		
Crunchy	85	2·1
Natural Wheat Germ	85	2·1
Cheshire Wholefoods Wheatgerm	90	0·9
Froment Stabilised Wheatgerm	95	0·8
Granose Wheatgerm	102	2·0
Jordans Natural Wheatgerm	100	0·5
Kretschmer Wheatgerm (lightly toasted)	100	0·6

Drinks Calorie Guide and Chart

Drinks Calorie Guide

Drinks do not supply you with dietary fibre and do little, if anything, to satisfy the appetite – mostly passing through the stomach in a matter of minutes. That is why, in terms of weight control, it is generally better to eat a piece of fruit than to drink the juice.

There are many drinks, however, which are calorie-free and can be consumed with absolute freedom. These are listed on pages 121–4. The drinks listed all supply calories, and these must be included as part of your daily total.

Because alcoholic drinks lack nutritional value, those allowing themselves a little alcohol while following the F-Plan are recommended to have a minimum 1,000 calories (or 850 in the special circumstances described in Chapter 3) of food and drink, and add the alcohol-supplied calories to this total. There are very few people who would not achieve a speedy weight loss on a fibre-rich 1,200 calories a day, for instance, so you can ensure your nutrients by eating sufficient food and then allowing that little extra calorie ration for alcohol.

Many of the drinks listed here are not particularly recommended for F-Plan dieters; but they are included on the basis that if you are going to feel deprived without any one particular food or drink, it is better to include a little, while slimming, than to put too much strain on your will-power. Here is what we advise:

Milk. Do try very hard to get into the skimmed milk habit – not only for convenience in slimming, but also for help in future weight control. Whole milk is very costly in calories. Furthermore, the cream is the fat of the milk, and these days we are all being recommended to cut down on fat intake for both weight control and health.

Fruit juice. When in need of refreshment, it is better to eat an orange than to drink a glass of orange juice, for reasons explained above. Again, this is a good habit to establish.

Bottled and canned non-alcoholic drinks. 'Soft drinks', as we tend to call them, are a major source of calorie intake from sugar. They supply calories which do nothing to satisfy our hunger. Nowadays there is such an excellent range of low-calorie soft drinks available that it seems a pity to squander calories on these products.

The drinks listed in this chart are calorie-counted in the quantities which will be most easily recognizable and convenient for most dieters.

Drinks Calorie Chart

	Calories
Aperitifs, per bar measure	
Campari (50ml)	**115**
Cinzano	
Bianco (50ml)	**80**
Rosso (50ml)	**75**
Dubonnet	
Dry (50ml)	**55**
Red (50ml)	**75**
Martini	
Bianco (50ml)	**75**
Extra Dry (50ml)	**55**
Beer, Cider and Lager, per ½ pint (284ml)	
bitter	**90**
brown ale	**85**
cider	**100**
home-brewed beer	**120**
lager	**90**
light ale	**75**
mild ale	**75**
non-alcoholic lager (e.g. Barbican)	**45**
pale ale	**90**
special brew lager (e.g. Carlsberg Special Brew)	**200**
Beverages	
cocoa, 1 rounded teaspoon (10ml)	**20**
drinking chocolate, 1 rounded teaspoon (10ml)	**20**
Horlicks, malted milk, 1 rounded teaspoon (10ml)	**20**
milk	
fresh, whole, pasteurized, sterilized, homogenized, longlife (UHT), or untreated farm milk, ½ pint (284ml)	**180**

	Calories
Beverages, *cont*.	
fresh, semi-skimmed (e.g. Light Gold), ½ pint (284ml)	**140**
fresh, skimmed (e.g. Sainsbury's Vitapint Skimmed), ½ pint (284ml)	**90**
dried, skimmed, 1 rounded teaspoon (10ml)	**10**
Ovaltine, 1 heaped teaspoon (10ml)	**25**
tea, without milk, per cup	**0**

Fizzy Drinks and Mixers	
All 'low-calorie' labelled drinks (e.g. Energen One Cal Drinks, Diet Pepsi, Slimline Tonic) contain negligible calories	
American ginger ale, 4fl. oz (113ml)	**40**
Bitter lemon, 4fl. oz (113ml)	**40**
Coca Cola	
6⅛fl. oz (185ml) bottle	**80**
11½fl. oz (325ml) can	**140**
dry ginger ale, 4fl. oz (113ml)	**40**
lemonade, ¼ pint (142ml)	**50**
orangeade, 4fl. oz (113ml)	**55**
Pepsi Cola	
6fl. oz (170ml) bottle	**70**
11½fl. oz (325ml) can	**135**
Schweppes Slimline Shandy, 8½fl. oz (241ml) bottle	**15**
soda water, per glass	**0**
tonic water, 4fl. oz (113ml)	**40**

Fruit Juices, per 4fl. oz (113ml) glass	
apple	**40**
grape	**60**
grapefruit	
bottled, sweetened	**65**
canned, unsweetened	**35**
canned, sweetened	**45**

	Calories
in a carton (e.g. Just Juice)	25
frozen, reconstituted	45
orange	
bottled, sweetened	70
canned, unsweetened	35
canned, sweetened	55
in a carton (e.g. Just Juice)	40
frozen, reconstituted	60
pineapple	
canned, sweetened	65
bottled, sweetened	65
tomato, bottled or canned	25

Fruit Squashes and Cordials, per fl. oz (28ml), undiluted	
blackcurrant	
cordial	30
health drinks (e.g. Ribena)	85
lemon	
barley water	30
squash or drink	30
lime juice cordial	25
orange squash or drink	35
whole grapefruit drink	30

Liqueurs, per bar measure	
Benedictine (25ml)	90
Cointreau (25ml)	85
Crème de Menthe (25ml)	80
Drambuie (25ml)	85
Grand Marnier (25ml)	80
Kirsch (25ml)	50
Tia Maria (25ml)	75

Port and Sherry	
sherry	
cream (50ml), small schooner	65

	Calories
Port and Sherry, *cont*.	
dry (50ml), small schooner	55
medium (50ml), small schooner	60
port (50ml)	75
Spirits, per bar measure	
brandy (25ml)	50
gin (25ml)	50
rum (25ml)	50
vodka, (25ml)	50
whisky (25ml)	50
Wine, per 4fl. oz (113ml) glass	
red	
dry	80
sweet	95
rosé	80
white	
dry	75
sparkling	90
sweet	100

Your Basic Calorie and Fibre Chart

Your Basic Calorie and Fibre Chart

In this chart calorie and fibre values are given per oz (28g) of food. More precise fibre and calorie figures are given here (as opposed to rounded figures in the other charts, which suffice when dealing with large total quantities).

Food	Calories per oz (28g)	Fibre g per oz (28g)
All Bran	70	7·9
Almond paste	124	1·8
Almonds, shelled, whole or ground	158	4·1
Apples eating, raw		
weighed with skin and core	10	0·6
flesh only	13	0·6
cooking		
raw, flesh only	10	0·7
baked or stewed without sugar	9	0·6
Apricots fresh		
raw, weighed with stones	7	0·5
stewed, without sugar, weighed		
with stones	6	0·4
dried		
raw	51	6·7
no-need-to-soak		
(e.g. Whitworths), raw	44	6·0
stewed without sugar	18	2·5
canned in syrup	30	0·4
Arrowroot	99	0·8
Artichokes, globe, boiled	4	0·3

Food	Calories per oz (28g)	Fibre g per oz (28g)
Asparagus, boiled	5	0·4
Aubergines, raw, flesh only	4	0·7
Avocado, flesh only	62	0·6
Bacon		
collar joint		
raw, lean and fat	89	0
boiled, lean and fat	91	0
lean only	53	0
gammon joint		
raw, lean and fat	66	0
boiled, lean and fat	75	0
boiled, lean only	47	0
gammon rashers		
grilled, lean and fat	64	0
grilled, lean only	48	0
back rashers		
raw, lean and fat	120	0
grilled, lean and fat	113	0
fried, lean and fat	130	0
middle rashers		
raw, lean and fat	119	0
grilled, lean and fat	116	0
fried, lean and fat	134	0
streaky rashers		
raw, lean and fat	116	0
grilled, lean and fat	118	0
fried, lean and fat	139	0
Baking powder	46	0
Bananas		
weighed with skin	13	0·6
flesh only	22	1·0

Food	Calories per oz (28g)	Fibre g per oz (28g)
Barcelona nuts, shelled	179	2·9
Barley, pearl		
raw	100	1·8
boiled	34	0·6
Bean sprouts		
raw	8	0·3
canned	3	0·8
boiled	10	0·3
Beans		
adzuki, dry weight	91	7·0
baked, canned in tomato sauce	18	2·0
black-eyed, dry weight	97	7·2
broad, boiled	13	1·2
butter		
dry weight	76	6·0
boiled	27	1·4
french, boiled	2	0·9
haricot		
dry weight	76	7·2
boiled	26	2·0
mung, dry weight	65	6·2
red kidney		
dry weight	76	7·0
boiled or canned, drained	25	2·3
runner		
raw	7	0·8
boiled	5	1·0
soya		
dry weight	112	1·2
boiled	37	0·4
Beef		
beefburgers, frozen		
raw	74	0·1

Food	Calories per oz (28g)	Fibre g per oz (28g)
Beef, *cont.*		
fried	74	0·1
brisket		
raw	70	0
boiled	91	0
corned, canned	61	0
forerib		
raw	81	0
roast	98	0
roast, lean only	63	0
mince		
raw	62	0
stewed	64	0
rump steak		
raw	55	0
fried	69	0
fried, lean only	53	0
grilled	61	0
grilled, lean only	47	0
silverside		
salted, boiled	68	0
salted, boiled, lean only	48	0
sirloin		
raw	76	0
roast	80	0
roast, lean only	54	0
stewing steak		
raw	49	0
stewed	62	0
topside		
raw	50	0
roast	60	0
roast, lean only	44	0
Beef sausages		

Food	Calories per oz (28g)	Fibre g per oz (28g)
raw	**84**	**0**
fried	**75**	**0**
grilled	**74**	**0**
Beetroot		
raw	**8**	**0·9**
boiled	**12**	**0·7**
Bemax (wheatgerm)	**97**	**2·1**
Bilberries, raw	**16**	**2·0**
Biscuits		
cream crackers	**123**	**0·8**
digestive		
plain	**132**	**1·5**
chocolate	**138**	**1·0**
ginger nuts	**128**	**0·6**
matzo	**108**	**1·1**
oatcakes	**123**	**1·1**
rye crispbread	**90**	**3·3**
semi-sweet	**128**	**0·6**
short-sweet	**131**	**0·5**
wafers, filled	**150**	**0·4**
water biscuits	**123**	**0·9**
wheat, starch-reduced crispbread	**109**	**1·4**
Black pudding, fried	**85**	**0·2**
Blackberries		
raw	**8**	**2·0**
stewed without sugar	**7**	**1·8**
Blackcurrants		
raw	**8**	**2·4**
stewed without sugar	**7**	**2·1**
Bloater, grilled, weighed with bones	**52**	**0**

Food	Calories per oz (28g)	Fibre g per oz (28g)
Bovril	49	0
Brain		
calf and lamb, raw	31	0
calf, boiled	43	0
lamb, boiled	35	0
Bran, wheat	58	12·3
Brawn	43	0
Brazil nuts, shelled	173	2·5
Bread		
brown	62	1·4
currant	70	0·5
Hi Bran	57	3·1
malt	69	1·4
soda, white	74	0·6
wheatgerm (e.g. Hovis, Vitbe)	64	1·3
white	65	0·8
wholemeal	60	2·4
Bread rolls		
brown		
crusty	81	1·7
soft	79	1·5
white		
crusty	81	0·9
soft	85	0·8
wholemeal (e.g. Allinson)	60	2·4
starch-reduced	108	0·6
Bread sauce	31	0·1
Breadcrumbs, white, dried	99	1·0
Broccoli tops		
raw	6	1·0
boiled	5	1·1

Food	Calories per oz (28g)	Fibre g per oz (28g)
Brussels sprouts		
raw	7	1·2
boiled	5	0·8
Buns, currant	85	0·5
Butter	207	0
Cabbage		
red, raw	6	1·0
savoy		
raw	7	0·9
boiled	3	0·7
spring, boiled	2	0·6
white, raw	6	0·8
winter		
raw	6	1·0
boiled	4	0·8
Cakes		
fruit		
plain	99	0·8
rich	93	1·0
rich, iced	99	1·0
madeira	110	0·4
sponge		
with fat	130	0·3
without fat	84	0·3
jam-filled	85	0·3
Carrots		
old		
raw	6	0·8
boiled	5	0·9
young, boiled	6	0·8
canned, drained	5	1·0

Food	Calories per oz (28g)	Fibre g per oz (28g)
Cashew nuts	**157**	**4·0**
Cauliflower		
raw	4	0·6
boiled	3	0·5
Celeriac, boiled	4	1·4
Celery		
raw	2	0·5
boiled	1	0·6
Cheese		
Baby Bel	80	0
Brie	88	0
Caerphilly	101	0
Camembert	84	0
Cheddar	115	0
cheese spread	79	0
Cheshire	95	0
cottage cheese	27	0
cream cheese	123	0
curd cheese	40	0
Danbo	98	0
Danish Blue	103	0
Double Gloucester	105	0
Edam	88	0
Emmenthal	115	0
Fetta	54	0
Gorgonzola	112	0
Gouda	100	0
Gruyère	115	0
Jarlsberg	95	0
Lancashire	109	0
Lymeswold	115	0
Mycella	110	0

Food	Calories per oz (28g)	Fibre g per oz (28g)
Parmesan	114	0
Philadelphia, soft cheese	90	0
processed, full fat	87	0
Quark		
less than 1% butter fat	22	0
less than 5% butter fat	33	0
less than 12% butter fat	47	0
Red Leicester	120	0
Roquefort	99	0
Sage Derby	112	0
skimmed-milk soft cheese	25	0
soft cheese, full fat	110	0
St Paulin	98	0
Stilton	130	0
Tome au Raisin	74	0
Wensleydale	115	0
Cherries		
eating, raw	11	0·4
cooking, raw	11	0·4
stewed without sugar, weighed with stones	9	0·3
glacé	59	0·4
Chestnuts, shelled	48	1·9
Chicken		
light meat only, raw	32	0
dark meat only, raw	35	0
light and dark meat mixed		
raw	34	0
no skin, boiled	51	0
no skin, roast	41	0
meat and skin, roast	60	0
Chicory, raw	3	0·4

Food	Calories per oz (28g)	Fibre g per oz (28g)
Chinese leaves	3	0·6
Chips, fried in deep fat	71	0·6
Chips (grill), frozen, grilled	40	0·6
Chips (oven), frozen, baked in oven	55	0·6
Chocolate drinking	102	0
milk	148	0
plain	147	0
Chocolates, fancy and filled	129	0
Choux pastry, cooked	92	0·4
Christmas pudding	85	0·6
Cockles, boiled, without shells	13	0
Cocoa powder	87	0
Coconut fresh	98	3·8
milk	6	0
desiccated	169	6·6
Cod fillets		
raw	21	0
boneless, baked	27	0
boneless, poached	26	0
boneless, steamed	23	0
fried in batter	56	0
frozen steaks, uncooked	19	0
steaks, fresh or frozen, grilled	27	0
smoked		
raw	22	0
poached	28	0

Food	Calories per oz (28g)	Fibre g per oz (28g)
Cod liver oil	252	0
Coffee		
ground, roasted, dry weight	80	0
instant powder or granules	28	0
Coffee and chicory essence	61	0
Coley		
raw	20	0
steamed, weighed with bones and skin	24	0
Condensed milk		
whole, sweetened	90	0
skimmed, sweetened	75	0
Corn oil	252	0
Corn-on-the-cob		
kernels only, raw	36	1·0
kernels only, boiled	34	1·3
Corned beef	61	0
Cornflakes	103	3·0
Cornflour	99	0·8
Courgettes		
raw	5	0·5
boiled	2	0·3
Cow's milk, fresh, whole	18	0
Crab		
boiled, meat only	36	0
canned	23	0
Cranberries, raw	4	1·2

Food	Calories per oz (28g)	Fibre g per oz (28g)
Cream		
double	125	0
half	35	0
single	59	0
soured	59	0
sterilized, canned	64	0
whipping	93	0
Crispbread		
rye	90	3·3
wheat, starch-reduced	109	1·4
Crisps, potato	149	3·2
Cucumber	3	0·1
Currants, dried	68	1·8
Custard		
egg	33	0
made with powder	33	0
Custard powder	99	0·8
Damsons		
raw	10	1·0
stewed without sugar	8	0·9
Dates		
dried		
no stones	69	2·4
weighed with stones	60	2·1
chopped and sugar-rolled	77	2·0
Dogfish (rock salmon), fried in batter	74	0·1
Dried milk, cow's		
whole	137	0
skimmed	99	0

Food	Calories per oz (28g)	Fibre g per oz (28g)
Dripping, beef	249	0
Duck		
raw, meat only	34	0
roast		
meat only	53	0
meat, fat and skin	95	0
Eel, stewed, flesh only	56	0
Egg		
whole, raw, without shell	41	0
boiled	41	0
fried	65	0
poached	43	0
Egg white, raw	10	0
Egg yolk, raw	95	0
Eggplant, *see* **Aubergines**		
Endive, raw	3	0·6
Evaporated milk, whole, unsweetened	44	0
Figs		
green, raw	11	0·7
dried		
raw	60	5·2
stewed without sugar	33	2·9
Fish fingers		
frozen	50	0·2
grilled without fat	50	0·2
fried	65	0·2
Flaky pastry, cooked	158	0·6

Food	Calories per oz (28g)	Fibre g per oz (28g)
Flour		
brown (85% extraction)	92	2·1
patent (40% extraction)	97	0·8
rye (100% extraction)	94	3·3
white		
bread-making (72% extraction)	94	0·8
household, plain	98	1·0
household, self-raising	94	1·0
wholemeal (100% extraction)	89	2·7
Frankfurters	77	0·3
Fruit gums	48	0
Fruit salad		
canned	27	0·3
dried, stewed without sugar	29	2·2
Gammon, see under **Bacon**		
Gelatine	95	0
Glacé cherries, see under **Cherries**		
Glucose, liquid	89	0
Goat's milk	20	0
Golden syrup	83	0
Goose, roast, meat only	89	0
Gooseberries		
green		
raw	5	0·9
stewed without sugar	4	0·8
ripe, raw	10	1·0
Grapefruit		
fresh		
weighed with skin and pips	3	0·1

Food	Calories per oz (28g)	Fibre g per oz (28g)
flesh only	6	0·2
canned in natural juice	11	0·1
canned in syrup	17	0·1
Grapefruit juice, canned		
unsweetened	9	0
sweetened	11	0
Grapenuts	99	2·0
Grapes		
black, raw	14	0·1
white (green), raw	17	0·3
Greengages		
raw, weighed with stones	12	0·7
stewed without sugar, weighed with stones	11	0·6
Groundnut (peanut) oil	252	0
Grouse, roast		
meat only	48	0
weighed with bone	32	0
Guavas, canned	17	1·0
Haddock fillets		
fresh		
raw	20	0
fried, weighed without bones	49	0
steamed, weighed without bones	27	0
smoked, steamed, weighed without bones	28	0
Halibut		
raw	26	0
steamed, flesh only	37	0

Food	Calories per oz (28g)	Fibre g per oz (28g)
Ham		
boiled, lean only	47	0
cooked and vacuum-packed	40	0
canned	33	0
Ham and pork, chopped, canned	76	0
Hare, stewed, weighed with bone	39	0
Hazelnuts, shelled	106	1·7
Heart		
lamb, raw	33	0
sheep, roast	66	0
ox		
raw	30	0
stewed	50	0
pig, raw	26	0
Herring		
raw, flesh only	66	0
coated in oatmeal, fried	66	0·4
grilled, flesh only	56	0
Honey, in jars	81	0
Horseradish, raw	17	2·3
Ice cream		
dairy	47	0
non-dairy	46	0
Jam		
fruit with edible seeds (e.g. raspberry)	73	0·3
stone fruit (e.g. plum)	73	0·3
Jelly		
packet cubes	73	0
made up with water	17	0

Food	Calories per oz (28g)	Fibre g per oz (28g)
Kidney		
lamb		
raw	25	0
fried	43	0
ox		
raw	24	0
stewed	48	0
pig		
raw	25	0
stewed	43	0
Kipper, baked		
flesh only	57	0
weighed with bones	31	0
Lady's fingers, *see* **Okra**		
Lamb		
breast		
raw, lean and fat, no bone	106	0
roast, lean and fat, no bone	115	0
roast, lean only	71	0
cutlets		
raw, lean and fat, weighed without bone	108	0
grilled, lean and fat, weighed without bone	104	0
grilled, lean and fat, weighed with bone	68	0
grilled, lean only	62	0
leg		
raw, lean and fat, weighed without bone	67	0
roast, lean and fat, weighed without bone	74	0

Food	Calories per oz (28g)	Fibre g per oz (28g)
Lamb, *cont.*		
roast, lean only	53	0
loin chops		
raw, lean and fat, weighed without bone	106	0
grilled, lean and fat, weighed without bone	99	0
grilled, lean and fat, weighed with bone	78	0
lean only	62	0
scrag and neck		
raw, lean and fat, weighed without bone	88	0
stewed, lean and fat, weighed without bone	82	0 .
stewed, lean only, weighed with fat and bone	71	0
shoulder		
raw, lean and fat, weighed without bone	88	0
roast, lean and fat, weighed without bone	88	0
roast, lean only	55	0
Lard	250	0
Laverbread (cooked, puréed seaweed, coated in oatmeal)	15	0·9
Leeks		
raw	9	0·9
boiled	7	1·1
Lemon curd		
starch base	79	0·1
home-made	81	0

Food	Calories per oz (28g)	Fibre g per oz (28g)
Lemon juice, fresh	2	0
Lemon sole		
raw	23	0
fried coated in crumbs, weighed with bones	48	0·1
steamed, weighed without bones	25	0
Lemons, whole, including skin	4	1·4
Lentils		
raw	85	3·3
split, boiled	28	1·0
Lettuce, raw	3	0·4
Liquorice Allsorts	88	0
Liver		
calf		
raw	43	0
fried	71	0
chicken		
raw	38	0
fried	54	0
lamb		
raw	50	0
fried	65	0
ox		
raw	46	0
stewed	55	0
Liver sausage	87	0·1
Loganberries		
raw	5	1·7
stewed without sugar	4	1·6
canned in syrup	28	0·9

Food	Calories per oz (28g)	Fibre g per oz (28g)
Longlife milk	18	0
Low-fat spread (e.g. Outline, St Ivel Gold)	102	0
Luncheon meat, canned	88	0·1
Lychees		
raw	18	0·1
canned	19	0·1
Macaroni		
white		
raw	104	0·8
boiled	33	0·3
wholewheat		
raw	97	2·8
boiled	32	0·9
Mackerel		
fresh		
raw	62	0
fried, flesh only	53	0
kippered, raw	62	0
hot smoked, as sold	70	0
Maize oil	252	0
Mandarin oranges, canned	16	0·1
Mangoes		
raw	17	0·4
canned	22	0·3
Margarine, all brands, hard, soft and polyunsaturated	210	0
Marmalade	73	0·2

Food	Calories per oz (28g)	Fibre g per oz (28g)
Marmite	50	0
Marrow		
raw	4	0·5
boiled	2	0·2
Marzipan	124	1·8
Mayonnaise	201	0
Medlars, raw, flesh only	12	2·9
Melon		
cantaloup		
raw, weighed with skin	4	0·2
raw, flesh only	7	0·3
yellow, honeydew		
raw, weighed with skin	4	0·2
raw, flesh only	6	0·3
water		
raw, weighed with skin	3	0·1
raw, flesh only	6	0·3
Milk		
fresh		
whole, pasteurized, sterilized, homogenized, longlife (UHT) or untreated farm milk	18	0
whole, Channel Islands	21	0
semi-skimmed (e.g. Light Gold)	14	0
skimmed (e.g. Sainsbury's Vitapint Skimmed)	9	0
condensed		
whole, sweetened	90	0
skimmed, sweetened	75	0
evaporated, whole, unsweetened	44	0

Food	Calories per oz (28g)	Fibre g per oz (28g)
Milk, *cont*.		
dried		
whole, not made up	137	0
skimmed (e.g. Marvel), not made up	95	0
skimmed with added vegetable fat (e.g. Cadbury's Pint Size), not made up	140	0
skimmed with added vegetable fat, made up with water	14	0
cultured buttermilk	10	0
goat's milk	20	0
soya milk, diluted as instructed	18	0
Mincemeat	66	0·9
Minestrone soup, dried	83	1·8
Muesli	103	2·0
Mulberries, raw	10	0·5
Mushrooms		
raw	4	0·7
fried	59	1·1
Mussels		
raw, weighed without shells	18	0
boiled, weighed without shells	24	0
Mustard and cress, raw	3	1·0
Nectarines		
raw, flesh and skin, no stones	14	0·7
raw, whole fruit weighed with stone	13	0·6
Oatcakes	123	1·1

Food	Calories per oz (28g)	Fibre g per oz (28g)
Oatmeal, raw	112	2·0
Okra (Lady's fingers), raw	5	0·9
Olive oil	252	0
Olives, in brine		
weighed with stones	23	1·0
weighed without stones	29	1·2
Onions		
raw	6	0·4
boiled	4	0·4
fried	97	1·3
spring, raw	10	0·9
Orange juice		
fresh	11	0
canned		
unsweetened	9	0
sweetened	14	0
Oranges		
whole, weighed with peel and pips	7	0·4
flesh only	10	0·6
Ovaltine	106	0
Oxo cubes	64	0
Oxtail, stewed, weighed on the bone	26	0
Oysters, raw		
weighed with shell	2	0
weighed without shell	14	0
Papaya (pawpaw), canned	18	0·1
Parsley, raw	6	2·5

Food	Calories per oz (28g)	Fibre g per oz (28g)
Parsnips		
raw	14	1·1
boiled	16	0·7
Partridge, roast		
meat only	59	0
weighed on the bone	36	0
Passion fruit (Granadilla), raw, weighed with skin	4	1·9
Pastry, *see* **Choux pastry, Flaky pastry, Shortcrust pastry**		
Pawpaw, *see* **Papaya**		
Peaches		
fresh raw, flesh only	10	0·4
raw, weighed with stone	9	0·3
dried		
raw	59	4·0
stewed without sugar	22	1·5
canned	24	0·3
Peanut butter	174	2·1
Peanut oil	252	0
Peanuts		
fresh	160	2·3
roasted	160	2·3
Pearl barley, *see* **Barley, pearl**		
Pears		
eating		
flesh only	11	0·6
weighed with skin and core	8	0·5

Food	Calories per oz (28g)	Fibre g per oz (28g)
cooking		
raw, flesh only	10	0·8
stewed without sugar	8	0·7
canned	22	0·5
Peas		
fresh		
raw	19	1·5
boiled	15	1·5
frozen		
raw	15	2·2
boiled	11	2·2
canned		
garden	13	1·8
processed	22	2·2
dried		
raw	80	4·7
boiled	29	1·3
split, dried		
raw	87	3·3
boiled	33	1·4
chick		
raw	90	4·2
boiled	30	1·7
red pigeon, raw	84	4·2
Peppers, green		
raw	4	0·3
boiled	4	0·3
Peppermints	110	0
Pheasant, roast		
meat only	60	0
weighed with bone	38	0
Piccalilli	9	0·5

Food	Calories per oz (28g)	Fibre g per oz (28g)
Pickle, sweet	38	0·5
Pigeon, roast		
meat only	64	0
weighed with bone	28	0
Pilchards, canned in tomato sauce	35	0
Pineapple		
fresh, no skin and core	13	0·3
canned	22	0·3
Pineapple juice, canned	15	0
Plaice		
raw, flesh only	25	0
fried in batter	78	0·2
fried in crumbs	64	0·1
steamed, flesh only	26	0
Plantain		
green		
raw	31	1·6
boiled	34	1·8
ripe, fried	75	1·6
Plums		
Victoria dessert, raw, weighed with stones	10	0·6
cooking		
raw, weighed with stones	6	0·6
stewed without sugar, weighed with stones	7	0·6
Polony	79	0·2
Pomegranate pulp	22	0·3

Food	Calories per oz (28g)	Fibre g per oz (28g)
Pork		
belly rashers		
raw, lean and fat	107	0
grilled, lean and fat	111	0
chops		
loin, raw, lean and fat, weighed without bone	92	0
loin, grilled, lean and fat, weighed without bone	93	0
loin, grilled, lean and fat, weighed with bone	72	0
loin, grilled, lean only	63	0
loin, grilled, lean only, weighed with fat and bone	37	0
leg		
raw, lean and fat	75	0
roast, lean and fat	80	0
roast, lean only	52	0
Pork sausages		
raw	103	0·1
fried	89	0·1
grilled	89	0·1
Porridge (oatmeal made up with water)	12	0·2
Porridge oats	113	2·0
Potatoes		
old		
raw, peeled	24	0·6
boiled	22	0·3
mashed	33	0·3
baked, weighed with skin	24	0·7
baked, flesh only	29	0·7
roast	44	0·6

Food	Calories per oz (28g)	Fibre g per oz (28g)
Potatoes, *cont.*		
chip, medium-thick cut	71	0·6
new		
boiled	21	0·6
canned, drained	15	0·7
instant powder		
dry	89	4·6
made up	20	1·0
crisps	149	3·2
Prawns, boiled, shelled	30	0
Prunes		
dried		
raw, with stones	38	3·8
no-need-to-soak (e.g. Whitworths),		
raw	33	3·4
stewed without sugar	21	2·1
Puffed wheat	91	4·3
Pumpkins, raw	4	0·1
Quinces, raw, flesh only	7	1·8
Rabbit		
raw, meat only	35	0
stewed		
meat only	50	0
weighed on the bone	25	0
Radishes, raw	4	0·3
Raisins, dried	69	1·9
Raspberries		
raw	7	2·1

Food	Calories per oz (28g)	Fibre g per oz (28g)
stewed without sugar	7	2·2
canned in syrup	24	1·4
Ready Brek	109	2·1
Redcurrants		
raw	6	2·3
stewed without sugar	5	2·0
Rhubarb		
raw	2	0·7
stewed without sugar	2	0·7
stewed with sugar	13	0·6
Ribena, undiluted	64	0
Rice Krispies	104	1·3
Rice		
brown		
raw	100	1·2
boiled	36	0·4
white		
raw	103	0·7
boiled	34	0·2
Rice pudding		
home-made	37	0·1
canned	25	0·1
Rock salmon, fried in batter	74	0·1
Roe		
cod, hard		
raw	32	0
fried	57	0
herring, soft		
raw	22	0
fried	68	0

Food	Calories per oz (28g)	Fibre g per oz (28g)
Rosehip syrup, undiluted	65	0
Rye crispbread	90	3·3
Rye flour	94	3·3
Safflower seed oil	252	0
Sago, raw	99	0·8
Saithe (coley)		
raw	20	0
steamed, no bones	28	0
Salad cream	90	0
Salami	137	0
Salmon		
fresh, raw	51	0
steamed, flesh only	55	0
canned	43	0
smoked	40	0
Salsify, boiled	5	0·3
Sardines		
canned in oil		
fish only	61	0
fish plus oil	94	0
canned in tomato sauce	50	0
Sausages, see Beef sausages, Pork sausages		
Saveloy	73	0·1
Scallops, steamed, no shells	29	0
Scampi, in breadcrumbs, fried	88	0·3

Food	Calories per oz (28g)	Fibre g per oz (28g)
Scones, made from white flour	104	0·6
Scotch pancakes (drop scones)	79	0·4
Sea-kale, boiled	2	0·3
Semolina, raw	98	0·8
Semolina pudding	37	0·1
Shortbread, made from white flour	141	0·6
Shortcrust pastry made from white flour		
raw	127	0·6
cooked	148	0·7
made from wholemeal flour		
raw	119	1·6
cooked	140	1·9
Shredded wheat	91	3·4
Shrimps boiled, shelled	33	0
canned	26	0
Skate, fried in batter	56	0·1
Skimmed milk, cow's fresh	9	0
dried	99	0
Soda bread, *see under* **Bread**		
Sole, lemon, *see* **Lemon sole**		
Soya bean curd	21	0·3
Soya bean oil	252	0
Soya beans, yellow, dried	112	1·2

Food	Calories per oz (28g)	Fibre g per oz (28g)
Soya flour		
full fat	125	3·3
low fat	99	4·0
Spaghetti		
white		
raw	106	0·8
boiled	33	0·2
brown wholewheat		
raw	97	2·8
boiled	32	0·9
canned in tomato sauce	17	0·3
Special K	109	1·5
Spinach, boiled	8	1·8
Sprats, fried, whole fish	109	0
Spring greens, boiled	3	1·1
Sprouts, brussels, *see* **Brussels sprouts**		
Strawberries		
raw	7	0·6
canned in syrup	23	0·3
Suet		
block	251	0
shredded	231	0
Suet pudding, sweet, steamed	93	0·3
Sugar		
demerara	110	0
white (caster, granulated, icing)	110	0
soft brown	110	0
Sugar puffs	97	1·7

Food	Calories per oz (28g)	Fibre g per oz (28g)
Sultanas, dried	70	2·0
Sunflower seed oil	252	0
Sunflower seeds	137	1·0
Swedes		
raw	6	0·8
boiled	5	0·8
Sweetbread, lamb		
raw	37	0
fried, coated in egg and breadcrumbs	64	0·1
Sweetcorn		
raw, kernels only	36	1·0
boiled, kernels only	34	1·3
canned	21	1·6
Sweet potatoes		
raw, flesh only	25	0·7
boiled, flesh only	24	0·6
Syrup, golden	83	0
Tangerines		
flesh only, no peel or pips	10	0·5
weighed with peel and pips	6	0·4
Tapioca, raw	100	0·8
Toffees, mixed	120	0
Tomato chutney	43	0·5
Tomato juice, canned	4	0
Tomatoes		
raw	4	0·4
canned	3	0·3

Food	Calories per oz (28g)	Fibre g per oz (28g)
Tongue		
canned	**60**	**0**
lamb, raw	**54**	**0**
sheep, stewed	**81**	**0**
ox		
pickled, raw	**61**	**0**
pickled, boiled	**82**	**0**
Treacle, black	**72**	**0**
Tripe		
dressed	**17**	**0**
stewed	**28**	**0**
Trout, brown, steamed, weighed with bones	**25**	**0**
Tuna		
canned in brine	**33**	**0**
canned in oil	**81**	**0**
Turnip tops, boiled	**3**	**1·1**
Turnips		
raw, flesh only	**6**	**0·8**
boiled, flesh only	**4**	**0·6**
Turkey		
raw		
meat only	**30**	**0**
meat and skin	**40**	**0**
roast		
meat only	**39**	**0**
meat and skin	**48**	**0**
light meat	**37**	**0**
dark meat	**41**	**0**
UHT milk *see under* **Milk**		

Food	Calories per oz (28g)	Fibre g per oz (28g)
Veal		
cutlet, coated in egg and breadcrumbs, fried	60	0
fillet		
raw	31	0
roast	64	0
jellied, canned	35	0
Vegetable oils	252	0
Venison, roast, meat only	55	0
Vinegar	1	0
Walnuts, shelled	147	1·5
Watercress	4	0·9
Weetabix	95	3·6
Wheatgerm	100	0·6
Wheatgerm oil	252	0
Whelks, boiled, no shells	25	0
White pudding	126	1·0
White sauce		
savoury	42	0·1
sweet	48	0·1
Whitebait, whole fish, fried	147	0
Whitecurrants		
raw	7	1·9
stewed without sugar	6	1·6
Whiting		
fried, coated in crumbs, weighed with bones	48	0·1
steamed, weighed with bones	18	0

Food	Calories per oz (28g)	Fibre g per oz (28g)
Wholemeal bread, *see under* **Bread**		
Wholemeal flour, *see under* **Flour**		
Winkles, boiled, no shells	21	0
Yam		
raw, flesh only	37	1·1
boiled, flesh only	33	1·1
Yeast		
bakers', compressed	15	1·9
dried	47	6·1
Yogurt, low fat		
natural	15	0
flavoured	23	0
fruit	27	0
hazelnut	30	0·5
Yorkshire pudding	60	0·3

Easy Hi-Fi Meals for Slimmers

Quick, convenient, *so* easy to make – here's a selection of ready-planned meals to show how very simple F-Plan dieting can be, and why so many slimmers have applauded the 'no fuss' factor. For those just starting the F-Plan there is a wide choice of more than two hundred ready-planned low-calorie high-fibre meals in the F-Plan diet book, to add to this selection.

HI-FI LIGHT MEALS

Vegetable and Lentil Soup with Wholemeal Roll

Calories **300**; *Fibre* **14g**

15·3oz (435g) can Heinz Vegetable & Lentil Big Soup
1 Allinson's Wholemeal Bread Roll

Heat the soup gently until hot. Serve with the wholemeal roll.

Toasted Date and Cheese Sandwich

Calories **300**; *Fibre* **11g**

1oz (28g) stoned dates
1oz (28g) curd cheese
2 slices wholemeal bread (1¼oz/35g each)
4oz (115g) eating apple, cored and cut into wedges

Chop the dates finely and mix with the curd cheese. Toast the two slices of bread on one side only. Spread the date and cheese filling between the two toasted sides of bread. Toast the sandwich on the outside. Cut into four and serve with the wedges of apple.

Toasted Sweetcorn and Chicken Sandwich

Calories **300**; *Fibre* 9g

2oz (56g) canned sweetcorn kernels, drained
2oz (56g) cooked chicken, finely chopped
1 tablespoon (15ml) low-calorie salad cream
salt and pepper
2 slices wholemeal bread (1¼oz/35g each)
½ carton mustard and cress

Mix the sweetcorn kernels, chopped chicken and low-calorie salad cream together to make the filling. Season to taste. Toast the two slices of bread on one side only. Spread the filling between the toasted sides of bread. Toast the sandwich on the outside. Cut into four and serve with mustard and cress.

Sweetcorn Scramble on Toast

Calories **300**; *Fibre* 8g

2 tablespoons (30ml) skimmed milk
2 eggs (size 4)
salt and pepper
3oz (85g) canned sweetcorn, drained
1 slice wholemeal bread (1¼oz/35g), toasted
1 teaspoon chopped fresh parsley

Beat the milk, eggs and seasoning together. Pour into a non-stick pan and stir in the sweetcorn. Heat gently, stirring continuously, until the egg is just set. Spoon on to the wholemeal toast and sprinkle with the chopped parsley.

Creamed Mushrooms on Toast

Calories **300**; *Fibre* **8g**

7½oz (213g) can Chesswood Sliced Mushrooms in Creamed
  Sauce
2½ level tablespoons (¼oz/7g) bran
1 tablespoon (15ml) Worcestershire sauce
1 slice wholemeal bread (1¼oz/35g), toasted
small bunch watercress

Heat the sliced mushrooms in creamed sauce gently. Stir
in the bran and Worcestershire sauce and serve on the slice
of toast. Garnish with the watercress.

Canned Blackcurrants with Yogurt and Biscuits

Calories **275**; *Fibre* **8g**

half 10·6oz (300g) can Ribena Blackcurrants in Syrup
2 tablespoons (30ml) low-fat natural yogurt
2 Country Basket Six Grains or Yogurt Biscuits

Serve the canned blackcurrants with the yogurt and biscuits.

Granny Ann Biscuits and Cottage Cheese

Calories **250**; *Fibre* **10g**

2 Itona Granny Ann High Fibre Biscuits
2oz (56g) cottage cheese with pineapple

Spread the biscuits with the cottage cheese.

Canned Blackberries with Yogurt

Calories **250**; *Fibre* **10g**

7½oz (213g) can Sainsbury's Blackberries in Syrup
2 tablespoons (30ml) low-fat natural yogurt

Serve the canned blackberries with the yogurt.

Pea & Ham Soup with Crispbreads

Calories **250**; *Fibre* **9g**

half 10½oz (298g) can Campbell's Condensed Pea & Ham
    Soup
2 Energen Brancrisp

Dilute the condensed pea and ham soup with an equal
volume of water and heat through in a pan. Serve with the
crispbreads.

Prunes with Yogurt

Calories **250**; *Fibre* **9g**

7½oz (213g) can Tesco Prunes in Syrup
1 level tablespoon (15ml) low-fat natural yogurt

Serve the prunes with the yogurt.

Apple and Date Dessert Bar and Yogurt

Calories **250**; *Fibres* **6g**

5·3oz (150g) carton low-fat natural yogurt
1 level teaspoon (5ml) liquid honey
2 level tablespoons (¼oz/7g) Meadow Farm Toasted Bran
1 Prewett's Apple and Date Dessert Bar

Spoon the yogurt into a dish. Stir in the honey and sprinkle
the top with the toasted bran. Serve with the apple and date
dessert bar.

Cottage Cheese with Apricots and Crispbreads

Calories **225**; *Fibre* **14g**

4oz (113g) carton Eden Vale Cottage Cheese with Pineapple
2oz (56g) Whitworths No-need-to-soak Dried Apricots
2 Energen Brancrisp

Mix together the cottage cheese with the chopped dried
apricots. Serve with the crispbreads.

Minestrone Soup with Crispbreads and Cheese

Calories **225**; *Fibre* **6g**

½ pint (284ml) Knorr Minestrone Soup
3 Ideal Bran Crispbreads
1oz (28g) Edam cheese
few sprigs watercress
1 tomato

Cook the soup as directed. Serve with 1 crispbread. Serve the remaining crispbreads with cheese, tomato and watercress.

Toasted Mushroom and Ham Sandwich

Calories **225**; *Fibre* **8g**

half 7½oz (213g) can Chesswood Sliced Large Mushrooms in Brine
1oz (28g) boiled ham, lean only
1 tablespoon (15ml) tomato ketchup or brown sauce
2 slices wholemeal bread (1¼oz/35g each)
½ carton mustard and cress

Drain the mushrooms. Chop the ham and mix with the mushrooms and tomato ketchup or brown sauce to make the filling. Toast the two slices of bread on one side only. Spread the filling between the toasted sides of bread. Toast the sandwich on the outside. Cut into four and garnish with mustard and cress.

American Bean Salad and Cottage Cheese

Calories **225**; *Fibre* 7g

half 1lb 1oz (482g) can Green Giant American Bean Salad
4oz (113g) carton Eden Vale Cottage Cheese with Onion
  and Peppers

Drain the American Bean Salad and serve with the cottage
cheese.

Peanut Butter and Cottage Cheese with Crispbreads

Calories **225**; *Fibre* 6g

3 Energen Brancrisp
½oz (15g) peanut butter
2oz (56g) cottage cheese
2oz (56g) raw carrot sticks

Spread the peanut butter on the crispbreads and top with
the cottage cheese. Serve with the carrot sticks.

Date and Fig Dessert Bar with Banana

Calories **200**; *Fibre* 7g

1 Prewett's Date and Fig Dessert Bar
6oz (170g) banana

Eat the dessert bar with the banana.

Canned Apricots with Ice Cream and Crunchy Topping

Calories **150**; *Fibre* **5**g

7¾oz (220g) Boots Shapers Apricots in Low-calorie Syrup
2oz (56g) (2 small scoops) vanilla ice cream
2 level tablespoons (30ml) Meadow Farm Toasted Bran

Top the canned apricots with the ice cream and sprinkle with the toasted bran.

HI-FI MAIN MEALS

Chicken and Mushroom Pot Noodle

Calories **400**; *Fibre* **9g**

1 pot Golden Wonder Chicken and Mushroom Pot Noodle
6oz (170g) slice cantaloup, honeydew or yellow melon

Make up the pot noodle with boiling water. Eat the melon
and follow with the pot noodle.

Boiled Bacon and Pease Pudding

Calories **375**; *Fibre* **11g**

half 7¾oz (220g) can Sainsbury's Pease Pudding
4oz (113g) Birds Eye Original Mixed Vegetables
3oz (85g) boiled collar bacon, lean only

Heat the pease pudding and cook the mixed vegetables.
Serve the pease pudding and vegetables with the lean bacon.

Rice and Sweetcorn Supreme

Individual portion with accompaniments:
Calories **375**; *Fibre* **17g**
(*Makes 3 portions of Beanfeast Supreme*)

1oz (28g) raw brown rice, per portion
1 packet Oxo Beanfeast Supreme
7oz (198g) can Green Giant Mexicorn Golden Corn, per
   portion
½ grapefruit

Cook the rice in boiling salted water for 25 minutes or until
tender, then drain well. Follow the cooking instructions and
cook the Beanfeast Supreme. Heat the sweetcorn and drain.
Mix the drained sweetcorn with the rice and arrange in a
ring on a serving plate. Divide the cooked Beanfeast
Supreme into three portions and serve one portion in the
centre of the rice and sweetcorn. Start or complete the meal
with the grapefruit.

Sausalatas and Beans

Calories **350**; *Fibre* **20g**

2 sausalatas from 10oz (283g) can Granose Sausalatas
7·9oz (225g) can baked beans with tomato sauce
1 slice wholemeal bread (1¼oz/35g), toasted

Cut the sausalatas into chunks. Add to the baked beans and
heat through. Toast the wholemeal bread. Serve the heated
beans with sausalatas on the toast.

Chipolata Sausages with Mushy Peas

Calories **350**; *Fibre* **16g**

2 pork chipolata sausages
half 10·7oz (304g) can Batchelor's Mushy Peas
half medium packet Cadbury's Smash Potato Pieces

Grill the pork chipolata sausages until well cooked. Heat the mushy peas and make up the Smash with boiling water. Serve the grilled sausages with the mashed potato and mushy peas.

Corned Beef Salad

Calories **350**; *Fibre* **15g**

half 1lb 1oz (482g) can Green Giant American Bean Salad
half 7oz (198g) can sweetcorn kernels
2oz (55g) corned beef, diced
2 tablespoons (30ml) oil-free French dressing
few lettuce leaves
1 Ideal Bran Crispbread

Drain the bean salad and the sweetcorn kernels and place in a bowl. Add the diced corned beef and the dressing and toss well together. Serve on a bed of lettuce. Serve the crispbread with the salad.

Chicken and Vegetables

Calories **350**; *Fibre* **14g**

8oz (227g) chicken portion
8oz (227g) pack Ross Mixed Vegetables (peas, carrot, sweetcorn, and cut beans)
2 tablespoons (30ml) thin fat-free gravy (optional)
half 8oz (227g) can Del Monte Pineapple Slices in Natural Juice

Grill or oven bake the chicken joint without added fat until well cooked. Cook the vegetables. Serve the chicken joint with the vegetables and gravy, if wished. Complete the meal with the pineapple slices and juice.

Beefburgers with Pease Pudding and Mushrooms

Calories **350**; *Fibre* **8g**

2 frozen beefburgers
half 7½oz (213g) can Pickering's Pease Pudding
7½oz (213g) can small whole mushrooms in brine
1 tablespoon (15ml) tomato ketchup or brown sauce

Grill the beefburgers thoroughly to allow much of the fat to cook out. Heat the pease pudding and mushrooms. Serve with the grilled beefburgers and the tomato ketchup or brown sauce.

Fish in Sauce with Vegetables

Calories **325**; *Fibre* **13g**

6oz (170g) packet Birds Eye Cod in Parsley Sauce
half 10oz (283g) can Smedley Broad Beans
7oz (198g) can Sainsbury's Young Carrots
2 Ideal Bran Crispbreads
½oz (15g) Edam cheese

Cook the cod in parsley sauce as directed on the packet.
Heat the broad beans and carrots and serve with the fish
and sauce. Follow with the crispbreads and cheese.

Spaghetti with Soya Bolognese

Per individual portion with accompaniments:
Calories **325**; *Fibre* **10g**
(Makes 3 portions of Bolognese Sauce)

2oz (56g) wholewheat spaghetti, per serving
1 packet Oxo Beanfeast Bolognese
1 level teaspoon (5ml) grated Parmesan cheese, per serving
1 tomato, sliced, per serving
1oz (28g) piece cucumber, sliced, per serving

Cook the spaghetti in boiling salted water until tender, about
15 minutes, then drain. Meanwhile cook the Beanfeast
Bolognese Sauce as instructed on the packet. Divide the
Bolognese Sauce into three portions and serve one portion
with the spaghetti. Sprinkle over the grated Parmesan cheese
and serve with a side dish of sliced tomato and cucumber.

Grilled Sausalatas and Mash

Calories **300**; *Fibre* **22g**

2 sausalatas from 10oz (283g) can Granose Sausalatas
½ medium packet Cadbury's Smash Potato Pieces
8oz (227g) Birds Eye Peas and Baby Carrots

Grill the sausalatas until thoroughly heated. Make up the
Smash with boiling water. Cook the peas and carrots. Serve
the sausalatas with the mashed potato and vegetables.

Ham and Pease Pudding Rolls

Calories **300**; *Fibre* **14g**

half 7¾oz (220g) can Sainsbury's Pease Pudding
2 – 3 slices (2oz/56g) cooked lean ham
half 10½oz (298g) can Sainsbury's Sliced Carrots
half 10oz (283g) can Sainsbury's Cut Green Beans
7¾oz (220g) can Boots Shapers Apricots in Low-calorie
   Syrup

Heat the pease pudding and divide between the slices of ham.
Roll the ham slice up with the pease pudding inside. Serve
with the heated sliced carrots and beans. Follow with the
can of apricots.

Bologna and Bean Salad

Calories **300**; *Fibre* **12g**

one-third 10oz (283g) can Granose Bologna
1 tomato, sliced
one-third 1lb 1oz (482g) can Green Giant American Bean
    Salad
4 black or green olives
2 Ideal Bran Crispbreads

Slice the Bologna thinly and arrange in a circle around a
serving plate. Pile the American Bean Salad in the centre.
Garnish with the sliced tomato and olives. Chill before
serving. Accompany with the crispbreads.

'Savoury Cut' Casserole

Per individual portion plus jacket potato:
Calories **300**; *Fibre* **11g**
(Makes 2 portions)

7oz (200g) potato for jacket baking, per serving
4·97oz (141g) can Farrow Giant Marrowfat Processed Peas
1 small onion, chopped
7oz (198g) can Sainsbury's Sliced Young Carrots
7½oz (213g) can Granose Savoury Cuts

Put the potato to bake in its jacket near the top of the oven
at 375°F (190°C/gas mark 5) for 45 minutes or until tender.
Cut the savoury cuts into cubes and place in a casserole with
all the sauce. Stir in the onion and drained carrots. Cover
with a lid or foil and cook near the bottom of the oven with
the potato. Add the drained peas 10 minutes before the end
of cooking. Serve the casserole with the baked potato.

Kidney Bean, Onion, Apple and Cheese Salad

Calories **300**; *Fibre* **10g**

3oz (85g) canned red kidney beans, drained and rinsed
2 spring onions, chopped
4oz (115g) eating apple
1 tablespoon (15ml) lemon juice
1½oz (40g) mature Cheddar cheese, diced
2 tablespoons (30ml) oil-free French dressing

Mix the kidney beans and chopped spring onions together in a bowl. Core and chop the apple then toss in the lemon juice. Add the apple, diced cheese and oil-free French dressing to the kidney beans and onion and toss well. Chill before serving.

Lamb Chop with Butter Beans and Tomatoes

Calories **300**; *Fibre* **10g**

5oz (140g) lamb chump chop
7½oz (213g) can butter beans
4oz (115g) canned tomatoes
half 10oz (283g) can Sainsbury's New Potatoes
2 teaspoons (10ml) mint sauce

Grill the lamb chop until well cooked. Heat the butter beans, tomatoes and new potatoes. Serve the grilled lamb chop with the mint sauce and vegetables.

Corned Beef and Tomato Bake

Calories **300**; *Fibre* **8g**

3oz (85g) corned beef, sliced
8oz (227g) can peeled tomatoes
1 tablespoon (15ml) dried onion pieces
1 teaspoon (5ml) Worcestershire sauce
salt and pepper
7½oz (213g) can small whole mushrooms in brine
half 10oz (283g) can Sainsbury's New Potatoes

Put the tomatoes, dried onion, Worcestershire sauce and
seasoning in a saucepan and simmer gently for 5 minutes.
Turn into a small ovenproof dish and top with the slices
of corned beef. Cover and cook in the oven at 400°F (200°C/
gas mark 6) for 15 minutes. Meanwhile heat the mushrooms
and potatoes. Serve the corned beef and tomato bake with
the mushrooms and potatoes.

Fish Fingers with Peas and Tomatoes

Calories **275**; *Fibre* **11g**

2 frozen fish fingers
half 10oz (283g) can Batchelor's Bigga Processed Peas
half 8oz (227g) can peeled tomatoes
half 14½oz (411g) can Sainsbury's Apricot Halves in Apple
   Juice
1 tablespoon (15ml) low-fat natural yogurt

Grill the fish fingers. Heat the processed peas and tomatoes.
Serve the fish fingers with the peas and tomatoes. Follow
with the apricots and yogurt.

Beanfeast Mexican Chilli

Per individual portion with accompaniments:
Calories **250**; *Fibre* **11g**
(*Makes 3 portions of Mexican Chilli per packet*)

1 packet Oxo Beanfeast Mexican Chilli
half 9oz (258g) can Smedley Chopped Leaf Spinach, per
   serving
half 14½oz (411g) can Sainsbury's Peaches in Apple Juice,
   per serving
2 tablespoons (30ml) low-fat natural yogurt, per serving

Cook the Beanfeast Mexican Chilli as instructed on the
packet. Divide the chilli into three portions and serve one
portion with the heated chopped spinach. Follow with the
peaches and yogurt.

Tuna, Tomato and Red Kidney Bean Savoury

Per individual portion: Calories **250**; *Fibre* **11g**
(*Makes 2 portions*)

8oz (227g) can peeled tomatoes
1 tablespoon (15ml) tomato purée
7·9oz (223g) can Batchelor's Red Kidney Beans
freshly ground pepper
¼ level teaspoon curry powder
7oz (198g) can Sainsbury's Tuna in Brine
4oz (115g) frozen whole green beans, per serving
2 Energen Starch-Reduced Bran Crispbreads, per serving

Put the contents of the can of tomatoes into a pan and break
down with a fork. Add the tomato purée, drained kidney
beans, ground pepper and curry powder and heat through.

Drain and flake the tuna, add to the tomatoes and beans and heat through. Cook the frozen green beans. Serve the tuna, tomato and red kidney bean savoury with the green beans and the crispbreads.

More about Penguins and Pelicans

For further information about books available from Penguins please write to Dept EP, Penguin Books Ltd, Harmondsworth, Middlesex UB7 0DA.

In the U.S.A.: For a complete list of books available from Penguins in the United States write to Dept CS, Penguin Books, 625 Madison Avenue, New York, New York 10022.

In Canada: For a complete list of books available from Penguins in Canada write to Penguin Books Canada Ltd, 2801 John Street, Markham, Ontario, L3R 1B4.

In Australia: For a complete list of books available from Penguins in Australia write to the Marketing Department, Penguin Books Australia Ltd, P.O. Box 257, Ringwood, Victoria 3134.

In New Zealand: For a complete list of books available from Penguins in New Zealand write to the Marketing Department, Penguin Books (N.Z.) Ltd, P.O. Box 4019, Auckland 10.

Look out for these from Penguins!

VOGUE NATURAL HEALTH AND BEAUTY
Bronwen Meredith

Nature is back in fashion! And this superbly illustrated book will enable every woman to use the natural approach to health and beauty.

In this companion volume to her bestselling *Vogue Body and Beauty Book*, Bronwen Meredith explains how to make the most of the natural elements at our disposal to the benefit of health, diet, vitality and looks. Health foods, yoga, natural remedies, spas, culinary and beauty preparations from fruits and vegetables, and *cuisine minceur* are among the many topics covered.

'[The] bible of the body' – *Bookseller*

VOGUE GUIDE TO SKIN CARE
Felicity Clark

Keep every inch of the skin of your body in glowing health! Here the Beauty Editor of *Vogue* shows you where your skin is most vulnerable; tells you when to get expert advice; analyses facial types; describes proper cleansing, freshening and moisturizing and the changes that age brings; and discusses specialized problems. There is a whole section on total body care – diet, exercise, depilation, hands and feet, tanners and protectors – written to help you understand what causes and alleviates skin troubles, plus an A–Z of common skin problems.

and

VOGUE GUIDE TO HAIR CARE
VOGUE GUIDE TO MAKE-UP
VOGUE BODY AND BEAUTY BOOK
VOGUE BOOK OF DIETS AND EXERCISE

Try these delicious Penguin Cookery Books!

QUICK COOK

Beryl Downing

This is a cookery book for victims of the twentieth century .. That is, for all those people who love eating but don't have much time to devote to actual cooking. Imagination, planning and economy are the thirty-minute cook's chief weapons – and as the recipes here confirm, that's a combination which will ensure exciting and varied meals for years to come.

THE CHOCOLATE BOOK

Helge Rubinstein

Enter the world of chocolate – the most luxurious, sumptuous (and sinful) of all foods. Here is a tantalizing selection of recipes – chocolate cakes, ice-creams, pies, truffles, drinks and savoury dishes galore. Both cookery book and expertly written social history, this is an anthology to treasure.

PICNIC
THE COMPLETE GUIDE TO OUTDOOR FOOD

Claudia Roden

'Wonderfully evocative and useful ... *Picnic* covers every sort of outdoor feast, from backyard to grouse moor, from Japan to the Middle East, from Ancient Greece to John Betjeman's 'sand in the sandwiches' – *Sunday Times*

SIMPLE FRENCH FOOD

Richard Olney

'The most marvellous French food to appear in print since Elizabeth David's *French Provincial Cooking*' – *The New York Times*

'There is no other book about food that is anything like it .. essential and exciting reading' – *Observer*

Try these delicious Penguin Cookery Books!

FROM JULIA CHILD'S KITCHEN

'Julia Child may be the most important person in the world of food' – Paul Levy in the *Observer*

'French bread, croissants, vacherins, quiches, crab dishes, good homely vegetables and soups, even the most elaborate dish achieves a startling simplicity when subjected to Julia Child's genius' – *Daily Telegraph*

FOOD WITH THE FAMOUS
Jane Grigson

Part cookery book, part social history, and always an unqualified delight, *Food with the Famous* relates cookery to life beyond the kitchen. Through recipes of their favourite dishes, Jane Grigson introduces us to such famous people as John Evelyn, Jane Austen, Proust and Zola.

MORE FOR YOUR MONEY
Shirley Goode and Erica Griffiths

'This collection of recipes and ideas aims to cut your weekly food budget but also to give you meals which are something special. It gives you the chance to challenge galloping inflation with hints on costing, using convenience foods and fuel saving so that the next price rise becomes a chance to show off your ingenuity instead of another crushing blow' - The Authors

COFFEE
Claudia Roden

This delightful book tells the story of coffee and includes information on the different types and blends, on roasting and grinding and on the various methods of making a superlative cup of coffee – plus a selection of mouth-watering recipes, from cakes to puddings and ice-creams.

A selection from the range of Penguin Handbooks

THE WALKER'S HANDBOOK
H. D. Westacott

Maps, tents, clothes, Rights of Way, National Parks, the law, shoes, boots, farmers, first aid – all you need to know to walk safely and happily round Britain.

THE PENGUIN BOOK OF SQUASH
Samir Nadim

This is a book for absolute beginners and for people who want to improve their game. Samir Nadim hopes that by following his step-by-step approach more people will play squash and play it well.

SKIN AND HAIR CARE
Linda Allen Schoen

Hundreds of questions of daily concern to everyone are answered in the three parts of this handbook, along with questions on special topics such as birthmarks, excessive hair, and cosmetic surgery.

GRANDMOTHER'S SECRETS
Her Green Guide to Health from Plants
Jean Palaiseaul

A mine of information about the folk lore, history and modern application of over 150 herbs and flowers, categorized in alphabetical order and illustrated with line drawings.